AUG 2 1 2013

Candlestick Charting
DeMYSTiFieD®

Wayne A. Corbitt

McGraw Hill

New York Chicago San Francisco Lisbon London Madrid Mexico City
Milan New Delhi San Juan Seoul Singapore Sydney Toronto

1 2 3 4 5 6 7 8 9 10   DOC/DOC   1 8 7 6 5 4 3 2

ISBN   978-0-07-179987-4
MHID   0-07-179987-7

e-ISBN 978-0-07-179988-1
e-MHID   0-07-179988-5

This publication is designed to provide accurate and authoritative information in regard to the subject matter covered. It is sold with the understanding that the publisher is not engaged in rendering legal, accounting, securities trading, or other professional services. If legal advice or other expert assistance is required, the services of a competent professional person should be sought.

—From a Declaration of Principles Jointly Adopted by a Committee of the American Bar Association and a Committee of Publishers and Associations

The MetaStock figures are used with permission.

McGraw-Hill books are available at special quantity discounts to use as premiums and sales promotions or for use in corporate training programs. To contact a representative, please e-mail us at bulksales@mcgraw-hill.com.

This book is printed on acid-free paper.

To Caitlin, Christian, Emily, and Dustin—as you each leave the nest and spread your wings, may you fly with confidence and always seek the wisdom of God.

About the Author

Wayne Corbitt is a Chartered Market Technician whose programming background has enabled him to work with a number of money managers over the past 13 years to automate their trading systems. He has also worked for a hedge fund as a Research Programmer and at the RIA level as an Investment Strategist and Managing Director. Wayne also actively trades his own account. This wide range of experience makes him uniquely qualified to help others reach their financial goals. He is the author of *All About Candlestick Charting*.

Contents

	Introduction	*vii*
CHAPTER 1	**The Case for Candlesticks**	**1**
	Buy and Hold Leads to Unnecessary Losses	1
	Trader Psychology	4
	History of Candlestick Charting	6
	Summary	7
CHAPTER 2	**Candlestick Charting in Technical Analysis**	**11**
	The Role of Technical Analysis in Trading	12
	Charting Styles	15
	Summary	20
CHAPTER 3	**Candlestick Construction and Basic Candle Lines**	**23**
	Candlestick Construction and Components	23
	Candle Types	26
	Summary	33
CHAPTER 4	**Candlestick Reversal Patterns**	**37**
	Strong Signal Patterns	38
	More Subtle Patterns	57
	Summary	74
CHAPTER 5	**Candlestick Continuation Patterns**	**79**
	Windows	80
	Tasuki Gaps	82
	Separating Lines	85
	Neck Lines	88
	Thrusting Lines	93
	Rising and Falling Three Methods	96
	Summary	99

CHAPTER 6	**Sakata's Strategies and Longer Term Candle Patterns**	**103**
	Sakata's Strategies	104
	Longer Term Candle Patterns	116
	Summary	126
CHAPTER 7	**Basic Technical Analysis**	**129**
	Trends	130
	Support and Resistance	139
	Gaps	150
	Summary	154
CHAPTER 8	**Candlesticks and Momentum Indicators**	**157**
	Momentum Indicator Basics	158
	Oscillators	158
	Summary	184
CHAPTER 9	**Candlesticks and Volume**	**187**
	Volume Patterns	188
	Money Flow Index	193
	Accumulation/Distribution Line	195
	Chaikin AD Oscillator	198
	Chaikin Money Flow	200
	Volume Percent Positive	202
	Summary	207
CHAPTER 10	**Weight of the Evidence—Trading Examples**	**211**
	Trade Presentation Format	212
	Summary	224
	Conclusion	*229*
	Final Exam	*231*
	Answers to Quizzes and Final Exam	*237*
	Index	*239*

Introduction

Trading is a business. Just as in the sports or corporate worlds, those that take the time to practice and prepare increase their chance of success. Ardent preparation is the key to navigating the markets successfully for profit. The goal of this book is to help you learn to read and understand the daily messages sent by the market. The more knowledge you have, the better you can prepare for whatever scenario the market presents.

Candlestick charting fits nicely into this environment. The broader picture provided by technical analysis is complemented by the deeper look into the mindset of traders that candlestick charting can provide. By combining these elements into a macro-micro combination, the macro messages sent by the market meld well with the micro messages given by candlestick charting. Defining candlestick charting as micro does not diminish its importance. On the contrary, the micro, or short-term, aspect of candlestick charting can allow a trader to enter trades or take profits much more quickly than those who rely on broad-based methodologies. In other words, using candlestick charts allows a trader to execute his or her plan with the precision of a surgeon's scalpel instead of a lumberjack's chainsaw.

No book on candlestick charting would be complete without a tip of the cap to the pioneers who brought this methodology to the United States from Japan. Greg Morris and Steve Nison did the early work in obtaining the early Japanese literature and working with their Japanese counterparts to translate and understand these concepts. The candlestick patterns and their names presented in this book are the result of their tireless work to introduce candlestick charting into the broader body of Western technical analysis.

I have attempted to complement their work by showing how candlesticks can be integrated with more widely used technical analysis methodologies and how to use candlesticks with more conventional technical analysis indicators. In this book you will not only learn about the messages candlesticks send regarding the mindset of traders, but you will also learn how to combine candlesticks with volume, momentum indicators, support/resistance zones, and trends. We will even examine some new indicators along the way. If you have read my first book, *All About Candlestick Charting*, you will notice that the layout of this book is similar. I believe that a beginner level book about candlestick charting has to have a logical progression where the building blocks are put into place before the integration of other techniques can be introduced. Regardless of your level of expertise in using candlesticks, I am confident you will find a wealth of useful information in this book to add to your trading arsenal.

How to Use This Book

This book demonstrates the depth of knowledge that candlestick charting provides and explains how you can use this methodology effectively to increase your odds of trading success. It begins by providing a basic knowledge of candlestick charting and the theory behind it and then progresses to a deeper discussion of technical analysis, which will give you extra tools to help you identify higher percentage trading opportunities.

Chapter 1 makes the case for technical analysis, which is the broad discipline of market analysis to which candlestick charting belongs. Chapter 2 shows how candlestick charting stacks up against other popular charting methods and why it is superior. Chapter 3 explains how to construct candlesticks and the data components needed. Chapters 4 and 5 demonstrate the various candle reversal and continuation patterns as well as the theories behind them. These patterns will be presented with their own diagrams and chart examples to show real-world examples. It is essential that you thoroughly understand the concepts in Chapters 1–5 before progressing to the remaining chapters.

Chapters 6–10 build on the basic foundation laid in the opening chapters. The tools and concepts introduced in Chapters 6–10 will help you uncover higher percentage trading opportunities by concentrating on candle patterns that are confirmed by other indicators. This is known as a "weight of the evidence" trading methodology, which will increase your chances of making successful trades. The concepts presented and discussed in these chapters include trends, moving averages, support/resistance, momentum indicators, and volume analysis. I will even introduce a couple of new indicators that I have developed and use in my own trading.

Throughout this book, you will also notice that the concept of risk is addressed. Any time a trader takes a position to attempt to make a profit in the market, he or she is exposed to an element of risk—which, simply stated, is the chance that money could be lost on the trade. By using the concepts of trend, momentum, and stop placement, a trader can control risk so that losing trades are not devastating to his or her trading account. Not every trade you make will be a winner, and successful traders always have well-defined exit plans to be executed when a trade turns against them. All of these elements will be combined in Chapter 10 when specific trading examples are presented.

By the time you have finished this book, you will be more confident in selecting trading opportunities that have a higher probability of success. Successful trading takes practice, patience, and discipline. By using the concepts presented in this book, you should have a solid foundation that will increase your chances of trading success.

Let's get started!

Chapter 1

The Case for Candlesticks

Congratulations. By purchasing this book, you have declared that you will no longer fall for the Wall Street myth of "buy and hold." While there are investments that perform well over longer periods, blindly holding on to stocks or commodities during steep declines is not necessary or wise.

CHAPTER OBJECTIVES

In this chapter, you will

- Uncover the Wall Street fallacy of "buy and hold"
- Recognize the value of becoming defensive when market conditions warrant
- Understand that trader psychology moves markets
- Learn a brief history of candlestick charting

Buy and Hold Leads to Unnecessary Losses

The buy-and-hold methodology benefited from the greatest bull market in U.S. history, 1982–2000. Even then, however, it was not necessary to "hold on" through the 1987 market crash, the 1998 Russian currency crisis, or the bursting of the tech bubble in 2000. Do you realize that as of December 2011, the

FIGURE 1-1 • Value of the S&P 500 Index
Source: MetaStock

Standard & Poor's (S&P) 500 Index was trading at the same level it was back in December 1998? So for all of the ups and downs, those that followed the Wall Street mentality for stock investment are at breakeven over a 14-year period, using the S&P 500 cash index as a benchmark (Fig. 1-1), which does not even keep up with inflation.

Of course some stocks outperformed while others have underperformed the broader market during that period, but from a pure benchmark index standpoint, the index value is virtually the same. The buy-and-hold philosophy evolved from the mindset of salespeople who made a living by convincing investors like mom and pop or the average Joe to hold their investments through the good times as well as the bad. The market climate has changed drastically over the past decade, however, as years of profits can now be wiped out in weeks. This is no longer the market environment in which your parents accumulated wealth. The current environment that features high-frequency trading, instantaneous news releases, and sovereign debt drama can be devastating to the average investor. In order to combat this mentality, it is necessary to take a more active role in managing your assets. This involves trading your account more than the talking heads on Wall Street would have you believe.

Within the investment world, the word *trader* evokes different reactions in different people. To some it is a way of life—entering and exiting trades based on a preset, tested methodology. To others it is a "bad" word, lumped in with *market timing* and *day trading*, but those are bad words only because the media and Wall Street declare them so. The fact of the matter is we are all traders because each position has to have an entry trade and an exit trade. The only difference among viewpoints is the length of time the position is held. While some positions can be held as briefly as a few minutes (day trading), others are held for days, weeks, or months.

The ability to get a read on the market and step aside during periods of market weakness is the key to accumulating wealth. Limiting losses in down markets is an often overlooked component to successful investing, especially for those that are managing their own retirement accounts for the long haul. In today's market, declines can be as sharp as 23 percent in a week and more than 27 percent in a month as the S&P 500 demonstrated in October 2008! Those that dutifully held on during the 2008 financial crisis lost more than 51 percent of their equity portfolio value using the S&P 500 as a benchmark. Holding on to positions because "they will eventually come back—they always do" makes very little sense. Do you realize that a loss of 20 percent in your portfolio requires a subsequent gain of 25 percent just to get back to even? Or that a loss of 40 percent requires a gain of 67 percent just to get back to your starting point? Those that "held on for the long haul" from the 2007 high to the 2009 low needed to more than double their money *just to get back to even*! In order to protect your own personal wealth, you need to step away from the buy-and-hold myth, which I refer to as "buy and hope." Being able to read the market conditions and to take action before major declines is like putting up an umbrella when it begins to rain. You see the storm clouds and feel the rain, so you instinctively put up an umbrella to keep yourself from getting soaked. Making adjustments in difficult markets can be that simple. The advantage of being able to adjust in adverse market conditions is very similar to a technique used by miners. Have you ever heard of the expression "canary in the coal mine"? This alludes to a trick miners used to alert them to toxic gases being emitted in the mine shaft. They would take a canary in with them, and any toxic gases that were present would affect the canary first, allowing the miners a chance to escape with minimal harm. The same concept of an early warning system can be employed when protecting your wealth.

By using the techniques in this book, you will have your own canary with you when you venture into the markets. It makes no sense to continue to "hold on" during the bad times when your own signals are telling you that there is trouble ahead. By being able to sell and step aside, apply hedge positions (by raising cash or using inverse exchange-traded funds [ETFs]), or simply enter short positions (make profits when the market falls), you will be in a better position to protect what you have worked so hard to accumulate instead of willingly accepting steep losses because "the markets always come back."

The tactic of stepping aside in unfavorable markets is called *market timing*, but that term has been used negatively by the high spin media machine. The term originated in 2003 as the name given to the illegal practice of mutual fund companies allowing favored clients to trade more frequently than the fund's prospectus allowed—in some cases even accepting trades after the market had closed. This resulted in more favorable pricing for these selected clients. The term's negative connotation to label those that choose not to hang on during painful market declines shows the length Wall Street goes to in an effort to discourage those that want to take a more active role in managing their own assets. While trying to catch every twist and turn in the market is indeed a fool's game and a recipe for disaster, there is nothing wrong with using robust, market-tested indicators to tell a trader or investor when the market is beginning to enter a period of sustained weakness.

When you have finished learning the concepts in this book you should be able to read market messages and react accordingly. While candlestick charting on its own typically gives short-term signals that last anywhere from two to five days, those signals can be given longer term meaning when combined with technical analysis. Candlestick charting can also provide a longer term perspective when used in the weekly time frame.

Still Struggling

Be wary of trusting the advice of "Wall Street pros."

When trusting anyone with portfolio advice, they should always have a way to manage risk of loss in the market with defensive plays such as raising cash or applying hedges. In many cases, the money of "Wall Street pros" is made by what they sell—and as the old saying goes "a bear market is bad for business." Always beware of those that encourage you to hang on or "buy more shares" when the market is in a full-blown downtrend. That mentality shows a lack of understanding of the devastating effect of protracted market declines on investment returns. By learning to spot shifts in market psychology, you will be in a better position to manage your own portfolio risk.

Trader Psychology

Becoming a trader is quite easy when compared to other moneymaking endeavors. The barriers to entry are low. There is a wealth of online brokers who just want you to fill out paperwork, fund your account, and begin trading. This is a dangerous path chosen by those who are out to make an easy buck, however. For example, the mentality surrounding Internet stocks in the 1990s was as irrational as the gold rush back in the 1800s. It seemed that all one had to do was buy any Internet stock and instant wealth was within his or her grasp. However those that hung around too long following the bursting of the tech bubble in 2000 found themselves wiped out. Why? Because the psychology of the market shifted from positive to negative, and they failed to detect it.

In today's market, the game has become infinitely more difficult due to the proliferation of high-frequency trading and seemingly daily government and central bank interventions to spur sluggish economic growth and save countries from insolvency. The bottom line is that in order to succeed as a trader— whether you do it for a living or aside from your main occupation—you must treat it as a business. That means controlling your risk exposure and identifying the psychological characteristics of the market by determining whether the "herd" is positive or negative. *Herd* is a word for the collective will of traders who make up the market. Fighting the herd is akin to swimming against a strong current in a river. You may survive for a while, but eventually you will be swept away by the persistent unrelenting flow of the current. The key to successful trading is quickly identifying the path of least resistance (whether up or down) and trading accordingly.

The herd is comprised of normally lucid people—you, me, doctors, lawyers, engineers, money managers, etc.—who trade their own accounts or the accounts of others. Something strange happens, however, when the herd begins to move. Emotion creeps into the decision-making process, which can cloud a person's ability to think objectively. The fear of being left behind and missing out on price gains is a strong emotion (greed) that brings traders into stocks and strengthens uptrends. The fear of loss can force normally rational people to sell positions, increasing the strength of downtrends. It is very easy to see stocks moving sharply in one direction or the other and be overcome by fear or greed. All traders have been subjected to these emotional swings at one time or another.

One trait of successful traders is their ability to remain objective. Traders who can remove themselves from the emotion of the markets typically have better success than those who don't. Today's trader is inundated with data points from every direction, from tick data to real-time news stories. The market's reaction to this instantaneous data can be as difficult to predict as the movements of a five-year-old on a sugar high. Getting wrapped up in these emotional roller coasters can lead to bad decision making that will deplete your trading account in a hurry.

The tools presented in this book will enable you to identify the psychology of the herd and to adjust your trading plan accordingly. This task will be accomplished through trend and momentum assessment, which means identifying the market's direction and the strength or conviction behind its movements. Within that broader framework, we will add candlestick pattern analysis. Candlestick patterns can alert a trader when a short-term reversal is developing or when the prevailing trend is ready to continue after a pullback or consolidation. For example, the formation of a dark cloud cover pattern in an uptrend is a warning that the uptrend may reverse. Conversely, the formation of a piercing line in a downtrend is a sign that buyers may be ready to enter the market and take prices higher. If you have never heard these names before don't worry, they will be covered in detail in Chapter 4. While the signals given by candlestick patterns are short term in nature, combining them with the broader backdrop of trend and momentum analysis can alert a trader when a longer term trade may be developing. This basic, yet effective analytical combination of trend analysis with candlestick patterns will provide a firm foundation so you can begin to trade successfully in any time frame, from intra-day to weekly.

History of Candlestick Charting

Candlestick charting has been in use for more than 200 years and is one of the earliest known forms of technical analysis. Munehisa Honma (or Sokyu Honma, depending on the translation) is credited with laying the foundation for the development of this charting method, which has withstood the test of time.

Honma was born Kosaku Kato in 1716 in Sakata City, Yamagata Prefecture, Japan. He was later adopted by the Honma family. Honma began trading at the local rice exchange in the port city of Sakata, about 220 miles north of Tokyo. Sakata was a key port for the rice market as merchants came from miles around to conduct business there. In fact, Sakata is still a very important port on the Sea of Japan to this day. Honma concentrated his trading on the rice cash market and the fixed rice market, which is where he began to build his fortune.

Later Honma went to Japan's largest rice exchange in Osaka and began trading rice futures. One of the great innovations that Honma developed was a communication network comprised of men on rooftops every four kilometers from Osaka to Sakata, a distance of almost 400 miles. These men would send signals up and down the line by using flags. This was an early method of gathering real-time data—or as close to real time as he could get.

After finding great success in the Osaka markets, Honma was promoted to the level of *bushi*, or samurai. He then moved to Edo (Tokyo) where he continued trading in the regional markets. Honma died in Edo at age 87.

Honma recognized the importance of analyzing the day-to-day price movements in the rice market and the subtle signals that can be given by these movements. He understood the value of gleaning information on the psychology of traders from the daily fluctuations in price data. He would also study price movements based on seasonality, or the time of the year in which these movements occurred. Honma's method of studying one day's price movement to predict the next day's price was named the *Sakata constitution*. His trading success along with his charismatic personality made him legendary in his own time—even feared. He was nicknamed "Dewa's long-nosed goblin" (Dewa refers to the area around Sakata).

Although Honma did not develop candlestick charting, his philosophies were instrumental in creating the basis of candle pattern recognition. He wrote 160 rules that were known as *Sakata's strategies*. It was from these strategies that candlestick analysis was born. The interpretation of most candlestick lines is influenced in one way or another by these strategies. We will examine some of these strategies, or price patterns, in Chapter 6. Some of these patterns resemble modern-day technical reversal patterns.

This ancient methodology has an advantage over modern Western charting styles because of its appealing appearance and ability to show intra-day data relationships effectively, most notably the relationship between opening and closing prices. A dark (or filled) candle body shows that the closing price was lower than the opening price, while a white (or hollow) candle body shows that the closing price was higher than the opening price. Figure 1-2 shows how candlestick colors illustrate the relationship between opening and closing prices. These differences in candlestick colors can give a trader a quick read on whether the efforts of buyers were stronger than those of sellers or vice versa during the trading day.

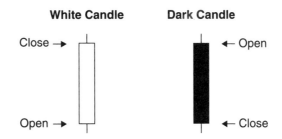

Candle colors reveal the open/close relationship.

FIGURE 1-2 • Candles and the Open/Close Price Relationship

In Chapter 2 a brief overview of technical analysis will be presented along with a comparison of the candlestick charting methodology with its contemporary peers. In subsequent chapters, we will delve deeper into candlestick patterns and the psychology behind them, and also show more modern technical analysis tools that can be combined with candlestick patterns to create reliable trading signals.

Summary

- Everyone is a trader in the market whether he or she admits it or not, since every position has to have an entry trade and an exit trade. Differences in philosophy can arise over the frequency of trades.

- The terms *trader* and *market timing* have been given bad connotations by Wall Street and the media. A trader is best described as one who does not simply buy and hold and thus does not leave his or her personal wealth to the whim of the markets. Market timing refers to using some form of analysis to know when to step aside as market conditions deteriorate and when to reenter the market when conditions improve.

- Trading is not a get rich quick scheme. It requires taking the time to understand the psychology of the "herd" and to know when to move in and out of the market.

- The herd is comprised of all who take positions in the market. Their collective will is what moves markets and creates trends.

- Successful traders remain as objective as possible and do not give in to the emotions of fear and greed.

- Candlestick patterns have short-term implications, but when combined with larger picture technical analysis, they can alert traders to longer term opportunities.

- The foundation for candlestick pattern analysis was laid by Munehisa Honma in the 1700s.

- Honma's trading methodology included a 400-mile communications network that consisted of men with flags on rooftops.

- Honma wrote 160 rules, known as Sakata's strategies, that influence the interpretation of most candlestick lines.

- Candlestick charting highlights the important relationship between opening and closing prices.

QUIZ

1. **Everyone is a trader whether he or she realizes it or not.**
   A. True
   B. False

2. **The key to accumulating wealth is**
   A. Buying and holding through good times and had
   B. Stepping aside during times of market weakness
   C. Listening to your broker
   D. Finding the best and latest hot tips

3. **The term** *market timing* **got its negative connotation**
   A. From the media, which used it to describe illegal trading by mutual funds
   B. As part of an effort to discourage those who don't want to buy and hold stock
   C. Both A and B
   D. None of the above

4. **In order to succeed as a trader, one must**
   A. Only spend an hour or two a week doing it
   B. Subscribe to the hottest newsletter
   C. Treat it as a business
   D. All of the above

5. **One trait of successful traders is**
   A. Having the instantaneous data feeds so they can react emotionally
   B. Having a knack for when and what to trade
   C. Their ability to receive tick data
   D. Their ability to remain objective

6. **Candlestick charting has been in use for more than**
   A. 20 years
   B. 50 years
   C. 100 years
   D. 200 years

7. **Who is the person credited with laying the foundation for candle pattern recognition?**
   A. Charles Dow
   B. Steve Nison
   C. Munehisa Honma
   D. Jim Cramer

8. **The emotions of fear and greed are good for a trader to have at all times.**
   A. True
   B. False

9. **The color of a candlestick represents the important relationship between**
   A. Opening and closing prices
   B. Opening and low prices
   C. High and closing prices
   D. High and opening prices

10. **The "herd" is comprised of**
    A. Insiders
    B. Major institutions
    C. All who take positions in the market
    D. None of the above

Chapter 2

Candlestick Charting in Technical Analysis

Technical analysis is the study of price movement. While the study of price movement has been done for centuries, technical analysis in its modern form (referred to as *Western technical analysis*) has its roots in the writings of Charles Dow around the turn of the twentieth century. Dow's writings led directly to the development of Dow Theory, which uses price movements in the Dow Jones Industrial Average in conjunction with price movement in the Dow Jones Transportation Average to determine whether the stock market as a whole is likely to move higher or lower. While Dow Theory was developed when railroads were the main form of transportation, its premise that the health of the transportation industry is a good barometer for measuring the growth potential for stocks is still widely used today.

CHAPTER OBJECTIVES

If this chapter, you will

- Understand the most basic application of technical analysis
- Learn where price charting fits into broader technical analysis
- Contrast the widely used methods of charting
- Understand the advantages of candlestick charting over other methods

The Role of Technical Analysis in Trading

Technical analysis differs from fundamental analysis in that fundamental analysis analyzes a company's financial statements while technical analysis analyzes that same company's price movement. While both methods have merit, there are still many on Wall Street who incorrectly categorize technical analysis as "reading tea leaves" or "reading chicken entrails." Nothing could be further from the truth.

One point that must be made regarding technical analysis is that it is not a crystal ball that allows a trader to know for certain what price will do. In other words, it should not be used to *predict* price movement; it should be used to determine what price is *likely* to do. Trading using technical analysis is an odds game where the gathering of evidence can help a trader make better decisions. The more evidence you collect, such as trend direction, momentum, and trader sentiment, the better chance of making a profitable trade. There are no guarantees in trading, however, so stop loss orders should be used on every position entered.

Broken down into its simplest form, technical analysis gives a graphical representation of supply and demand. Rising prices show that demand for shares or contracts is stronger than the supply of shares or contracts presented for sale, while falling prices show that the supply of shares ready for sale is higher than the demand generated by willing buyers. Price will continue to move in one direction or the other until a state of equilibrium is reached between supply and demand. Sustained differences in supply and demand cause price trends, or the tendency of prices to move in a specific direction (either up or down) over time as the actions of the herd take over, as discussed in Chapter 1. Whether for stocks, bonds, or commodity contracts, an accurate picture of how a security or commodity is perceived by traders can be gleaned by examining price movement over time. The key in using technical analysis properly is not to take a look at a single day's action and make a determination as to whether price is likely to move higher or lower, but to look at the price performance over time to determine the *pattern* of buyers and sellers. Buying or selling patterns can be ascertained by using price data in conjunction with volume data.

Volume shows the number of shares or contracts that changed hands during the trading day. The addition of volume into technical analysis provides a measurement of the amount of conviction behind a price move. For example, increasing volume on a downward price move shows increasing conviction among sellers, while increasing volume as price rises shows more conviction among buyers. The daily chart of Google Inc. (Fig. 2-1) shows an example of a change in the price/volume pattern that gave clues that a change in price direction was near. Notice how the formation of a doji (introduced in Chapter 3) was followed by a price decline on increasing volume. This showed that sellers were becoming more active and that the uptrend in Google's price was over. The role of volume in technical analysis will be covered in more detail in Chapter 9.

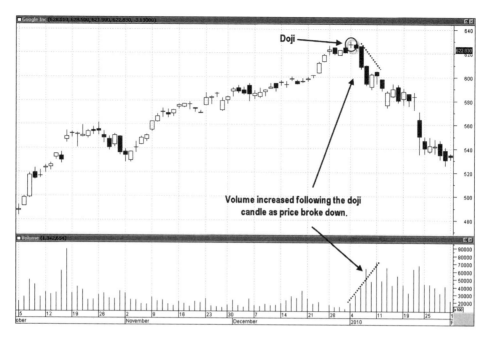

FIGURE 2-1 • Change in Price Direction for Google Inc., Daily
Source: MetaStock

Perhaps the most important aspect of technical analysis is its ability to help traders manage risk. Managing risk is paramount to the survival of traders in the markets. When the market mood or sentiment changes, the risk of loss increases for those who followed the previous trend. When positions are established on the assumption that the prevailing pattern will continue, the main risk to traders is that the pattern will change and the price direction will reverse. Look at the daily chart of Google in Fig. 2-2. Notice that this chart covers the same time period, only this time a trend line has been added. This is another piece of evidence that can show a trader when the market environment has changed. So now we have a doji candle that signifies a reversal in price, followed by a fall in price on an increase in volume. When we add the trend line to our analysis, we have a potent combination of indicators that increase the odds that price is about to reverse lower in a meaningful way. Trend lines are covered in more detail in Chapter 7.

The chart in Fig. 2-2 shows how effective basic technical analysis tools can be in helping a trader manage risk. This begs the next question: Why don't more traders or even longer term "investors" take advantage of such simple tools that can be their own canary in the coal mine? If a trader had a position in Google, why would that investor sit idly and watch his or her position value drop almost 100 points, or 15 percent, over a four-week period? That is such a needless, nerve-wracking exercise.

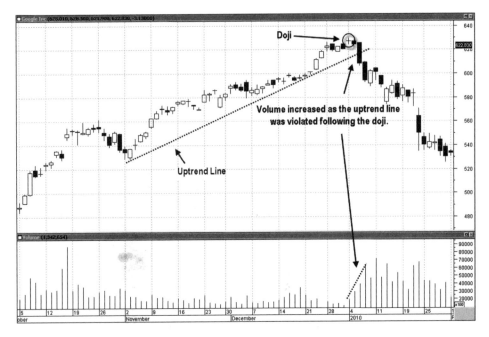

FIGURE 2-2 • Trend Line Violation for Google Inc., Daily
Source: MetaStock

In addition to the risk of trend reversal, there are two other types of risk at work when a person decides to buy and hold. First, there is the risk of draw-down, which measures the drop from the high value in your account (peak) to your subsequent lowest value (trough). Granted, if you hold on to the Google position in the above example it is an unrealized loss, but it is a loss in your account value just the same. In fact, in this case many traders become investors as they hope that Google can make it back up to its previous high point. This is why many "investments" are merely trades that have gone wrong. One high drawdown can cripple a trading account, and more than one can be devastating. Remember from Chapter 1 that following a loss or drawdown of 20 percent, it takes a subsequent gain of 25 percent *just to get your dollar value back to where it was before the drawdown occurred*. Sitting through monster declines like that does not demonstrate prudent risk management. The second type of risk in the buy-and-hold mentality is the risk of lost opportunity. What if the trader had sold Google when the trend line was violated on increasing volume and put that money into something else, or even just left it in cash? Had the trader acted at the lowest trading price on the day that the trend line was violated, that action would have resulted in a loss of only 3.6 percent from the high instead of the 15 percent decline that the buy and holder had to endure. The active trader would have kept an extra 11–12 percent of trading capital in his or her account instead of hoping for Google to come back fol-lowing the brutal sell off.

Mastering the art of technical analysis takes much practice. While the simple tools presented here can help a trader stay out of serious trouble, there are many other nuances that a technician learns over time. First, one must always be mindful of the overall market trend, as most stocks follow the trend of the broader market. Those that trade with the intent of holding positions for weeks or even months can benefit more from broader market analysis than by only looking at one or two individual stock charts. Being aware of the herd's mindset is always key to making great trades. While you will learn techniques in this book to allow you to jump on reversals quickly for profit, being mindful of the larger degree trend can mean the difference between a winning or losing trade. (Technical analysis will be discussed in much more detail in Chapter 7.)

Still Struggling?

Wall Street still downplays the importance of technical analysis.

This has been an issue for many years as those that are hard-core fundamental analysts continue to disrespect the role of technical analysis in trading. Their main argument is that you cannot use past price movement to predict the future. Yet, when it comes to applying methodologies, fundamentalists do the same thing with financial data. They use old data (past earnings, revenue, etc.) as a basis for their own analyses to determine the likely trend for earnings and revenue. While fundamental analysis has value, I liken the application of pure fundamental analysis to a person who has found a new shiny golden egg. The person takes it around and shows friends how shiny the golden egg is and listens to the platitudes of how intelligent a discovery it was. However when the person is asked when the egg will hatch (when will company shares begin to move higher in price to make a profit), that person doesn't know. Technical analysis shows when supply-and-demand dynamics have changed, alerting the trader when new buyers have also discovered the shiny golden egg, which will increase demand and drive the price higher. Using technical analysis can help a trader time his or her entry into a position so that the trader is not tying up trading funds for long periods waiting for a golden egg to hatch.

Charting Styles

A chart is a tool used by a technician to graphically display price information about a security. Choosing the right charting style for you is a purely personal decision. The goal of chart reading is to gather as much information about a security or commodity (price direction, trader conviction, etc.) in as little time as possible. Each chart examples that follows shows the same security over the same time period, which will give you an apples-to-apples comparison. Three of the four examples will contain a plot of volume as well. The four examples presented are the most popular charting styles used by technicians today.

Line Chart

A line chart (Fig. 2-3) displays only the closing price for each time period, with subsequent closing prices connected by a single line. The theory behind using this type of chart is that the closing price contains the sum of all trading activity during the trading day, with all other activity being looked upon as nothing more than "noise" or meaningless price gyrations. One of the drawbacks of using a line chart, however, is that the trader can miss out on seeing intra-day price reversals, which can help determine support or resistance areas. (Support and resistance are discussed in Chapter 6.)

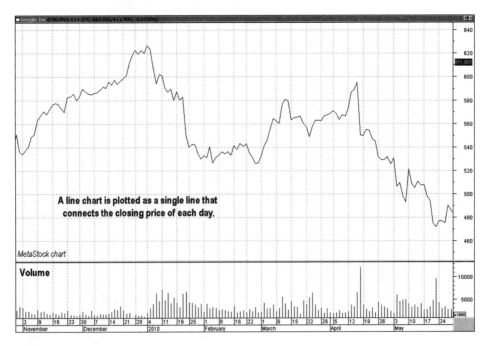

FIGURE 2-3 • Line Chart for Google Inc., Daily
Source: MetaStock

Point and Figure Chart

A point and figure chart consists of columns of X's and O's that represent price movements. This charting method uses only the high and/or low price in its construction; therefore, it is more focused on the daily extremes than on the closing price. The benefits of this charting methodology are that it shows support and resistance levels more clearly and makes for easier drawing and interpretation of trend lines. There are a couple of drawbacks to using this method, however. First, its construction is only concerned with price movements above or below price levels regardless of when they occur. This eliminates the element of time, which is important to anyone who does any form of cycle or time comparison analysis. Second, the point and figure chart does not allow for the inclusion of volume, thus robbing the chartist of the important sentiment measuring characteristics that volume can provide. Nevertheless, point and figure charting still has a dedicated following of technicians that appreciate its emphasis on pure price movement. Figure 2-4 shows an example of a point and figure chart.

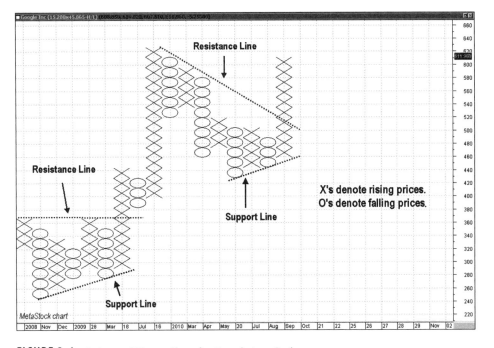

FIGURE 2-4 • Point and Figure Chart for Google Inc., Daily

Source: MetaStock

Bar Chart

The bar chart is perhaps the most commonly used form of charting and has been the industry standard for decades. With candlestick charting increasing in popularity, though, the bar chart's status as the industry standard may be changing.

A bar chart consists of individual bars for each trading period, with Fig. 2-5 showing daily bars. Each bar is constructed using the open, high, low, and closing prices. Bar charts show much more data at a glance than line or point and figure charts. Bar charts also allow for the proper plotting of volume for each time period, which adds another layer to the technician's market analysis. Since the bar chart shows both opening and closing prices for the period, it is possible to see whether buying or selling pressure was stronger for the day.

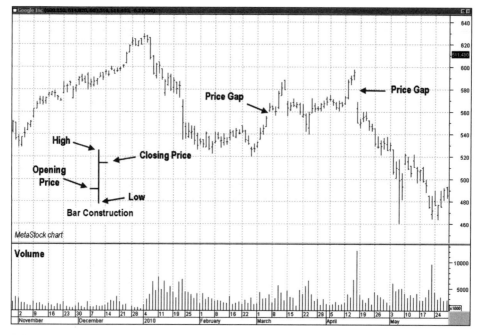

FIGURE 2-5 • Bar Chart for Google Inc., Daily
Source: MetaStock

Another advantage of bar charts is that they show price *gaps*, or blank spots on charts where no trading occurred between the closing of one day and the opening of the next day. Gaps are caused by emotional events that are typically tied to earnings reports, news specific to an individual stock, or broad-based market news that affects all stocks, such as economic data or Federal Reserve actions.

Candlestick Chart

The candlestick chart also uses the open, high, low, and close prices for the day but takes the bar chart one step further by enhancing the very important open-close relationship for the trading day. The visual aspect of candlestick charts causes them to almost jump off the page at a trader, offering more information than the standard bar chart. Figure 2-6 uses the same data as the bar chart in Fig. 2-5, but notice how much more discernible the daily patterns are because of the color contrast between dark and white candles. Most candlestick charting packages show candlesticks with different colors, but for the purposes of this book, black candles will be used when the close is lower than the open, and white candles will be used when the close is higher than the open. Also notice how the three high points in the chart were marked by reversal candles, such as the doji, spinning top, and the dark cloud cover. Each of these reversal patterns and the psychology behind them will be discussed in Chapter 4.

Candlestick charts also show price gaps just as bar charts do. But in candlestick charting these gaps are referred to as *windows* that are opened and closed

FIGURE 2-6 • Candlestick Chart for Google Inc., Daily

Source: MetaStock

by price action. Note the two windows in Fig. 2-6. When a gap is formed as price moves higher, it is referred to as a *rising window*. When a gap is formed as price moves lower, it is referred to as a *falling window*.

Candlestick charting has three distinct advantages over bar charts:

Readability—Candlestick charts highlight the important relationship between opening and closing prices. Although this relationship has short-term implications, when observed over time it can alert a trader when a larger scale price move or reversal may be developing.

Quicker interpretation of market psychology—Are black candles more prevalent than white candles or vice versa? That alone can tell a trader whether a market is under accumulation or distribution. Reversal or continuation patterns are spotted more readily because of the color contrast between positive and negative days. Once again, Fig. 2-6 shows the three reversal candles (doji, spinning top, and dark cloud cover). Would those potential reversal signals have been spotted as easily on a bar chart? Probably not.

Specific patterns that give insight into market sentiment—If a doji is formed following a downtrend and a long white candle forms immediately after, that is a sign trader sentiment is changing and higher prices can be expected. Conversely, a doji that forms in an uptrend immediately followed by a long black candle is a signal sellers are becoming more active and lower prices can be expected. A wide array of candlestick patterns can demonstrate how the supply and demand picture is shaping up. These patterns will be examined in great detail in Chapters 4 and 5.

Summary

- Western technical analysis has its roots in the writings of Charles Dow around the turn of the twentieth century.
- Technical analysis is not a crystal ball. It shows what price is likely to do, not what it will do.
- Technical analysis is a graphical representation of supply and demand.
- Volume is important to measure the trader conviction behind price moves.
- The most important aspect of technical analysis is that it helps traders manage risk.
- The type of charting style a trader uses is a personal decision.
- The point and figure chart only uses price extremes in its construction. Time and volume are not considered.
- Line charts only use the closing price for the day or time period being plotted.
- Bar charts and candlestick charts use the same price data points—open, high, low, and close.
- Candlestick charts provide more at-a-glance information than standard bar charts, giving the trader a quicker read on market sentiment and possible turning points.

QUIZ

1. **Technical analysis is used for**
   A. Predicting price movement
   B. Determining what price is likely to do
   C. Giving a graphical representation of supply and demand
   D. Both B and C

2. **Western technical analysis has its origins in the writings of:**
   A. Munehisa Honma
   B. Charles Dow
   C. Greg Morris
   D. Albert Einstein

3. **A price trend is best defined as**
   A. The conflict of the emotions of fear and greed
   B. Trader indecision
   C. The tendency of price to move in a specific direction over time
   D. None of the above

4. **Volume is used to measure**
   A. The number of shares or contracts traded during the trading day
   B. The conviction level among traders
   C. The amount of greed in the market
   D. Both A and B

5. **What two types of risk are not addressed by the buy-and-hold methodology?**
   A. Diversification and overlay
   B. Drawdown and lost opportunity
   C. Conservative and excessiveness
   D. None of the above

6. **Which charting style does not allow for the accurate plotting of volume?**
   A. Line chart
   B. Bar chart
   C. Point and figure chart
   D. Candlestick chart

7. **Which two charting styles use the same data points in their construction?**
   A. Line and bar
   B. Point and figure and bar
   C. Line and candlestick
   D. Bar and candlestick

8. **Which charting style eliminates the element of time?**
   A. Line
   B. Bar
   C. Point and figure
   D. Candlestick

9. **What are some of the advantages of candlestick charts over bar charts?**
   A. Readability
   B. Quicker interpretation of market psychology
   C. Specific patterns that give insight into market sentiment
   D. All of the above

10. **What is perhaps the most important role of technical analysis?**
    A. Determine the best asset mix
    B. Address diversification issues
    C. Help manage risk
    D. All of the above

Candlestick Construction and Basic Candle Lines

In Chapter 2 different charting styles were explained and contrasted, showing their advantages and drawbacks. This chapter looks at how candlesticks are drawn and shows the meaning of various candle lines.

CHAPTER OBJECTIVES

In this chapter, you will

- Learn how to use data points in candlestick construction
- Understand components used in candlestick construction
- Recognize candle color and body size and their meanings
- Identify classifications of basic candle lines

Candlestick Construction and Components

The most common comparison between charting styles today typically compares bar charts and candlestick charts. Bar charts still have a very loyal following but, as discussed in Chapter 2, candlestick charts are gaining ground because of their visual appeal, quicker interpretation of market psychology, and specific identifiable patterns that give insight into the shifting of trader sentiment. In this chapter we will introduce the components of a candlestick and then explain different types of candlestick lines and their meanings. A number of candlestick lines are discussed here, and you should learn these lines before moving forward. These basic candle lines form the foundation of candlestick interpretation and will be used to analyze more complex patterns in Chapters 4 and 5.

Candlestick charting uses the same data points (open, high, low, and close) as bar charts. The difference is in the construction of the chart lines. Since a candlestick chart highlights the difference between the opening and closing prices for each trading day, it gives a quick report of who won the trading day between buyers and sellers. While the same data points are also present on a bar chart, the open/close relationship is not as easily discerned. Figure 3-1 shows the comparison between a bar chart line and a candlestick line.

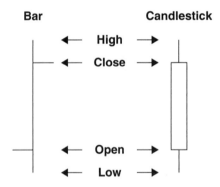

FIGURE 3-1 • Comparison Between a Bar Chart Line and a Candlestick Chart Line

The *real body* (Fig. 3-2) is the portion of the candlestick that lies between the opening price and the closing price. A dark (or filled) candle body shows that the closing price was lower than the opening price, while a white (or hollow) candle shows that the closing price was higher than the opening price. This relationship is further enhanced because of the width of the real body, which makes the difference between opening and closing prices more readily apparent. If a trader sees more dark candles on a chart, that is evidence of intra-day price weakness, which is bearish. If, on the other hand, the trader notices more white candles than dark candles, that is evidence that buyers were more active between the open and the close, which is bullish. Longer real bodies show more conviction among traders during the trading day, while shorter real bodies show indecision as the opening and closing prices were not very far apart.

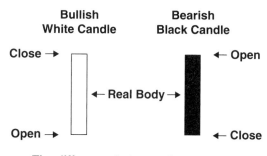

**The difference between the open and
the close is known as the real body.**

FIGURE 3-2 • Real Bodies in White and Black Candles

Shadows (or wicks) (Fig. 3-3) are thin lines above and below the real body of the candle that represent the price movement outside of the range of the real body. The shadow above the real body is called the *upper shadow*, while the shadow below the real body is called the *lower shadow*. The highest point of the upper shadow represents the high price for the day while the lowest point of the lower shadow represents the lowest price for the day. Long shadows with small real bodies represent indecision among traders as prices reached extremes in either direction, but the closing price was not much different than the opening price. Long upper shadows are seen as bearish since the price closed well off of the price high for the day, while long lower shadows are viewed bullishly because the price closed well off of the extreme low price for the day. Short candles with long shadows that appear in trending markets are typically viewed as early warning signals that a reversal in trend may be imminent. Examples of these types of candles are the doji and spinning top, which will be discussed later in this chapter.

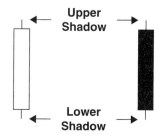

**Shadows represent the upper and
lower extremes for the period.**

FIGURE 3-3 • Shadows

Candle Types

Single candlestick lines can be categorized by their appearance. Their classification is determined by comparing the candle to its most recent 10 candles or so. Also, if a candle is formed that is much larger than anything over the last few weeks, traders should take notice because something is changing in the market. For example, was the real body long or short compared with recent candles? Were the shadows longer or shorter? Each category or classification has implications for who is in control of the market—buyers or sellers. In each of these classifications, notice the description of the size of the real body and also of the length of the shadows and how they are used to gauge the sentiment of the market. Multiline candlestick patterns will be covered in Chapters 4 and 5.

Long Candles

A *long candle* (Fig. 3-4), or a long day, is defined as a wide gap between the opening and closing prices, forming a long real body. The length of the real body is compared to recent candles, usually the most recent two weeks (or 10 candles). Long candles show conviction among traders as price moved decisively in one direction following the market open. A long white candle shows that buyers were more active as the closing price was well above the opening price. A long black candle is bearish since the price closed well below its open. In an uptrending market, a long white candle confirms the trend, while in a downtrend it could be an early sign of a trend reversal. A long black candle in a downtrend confirms the downtrend, while a long black candle in an uptrend may be an early sign of a trend reversal.

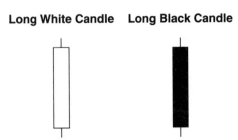

Long White Candle   Long Black Candle

Long candles signify dominance by either buyers or sellers, depending on the color.

FIGURE 3-4 • Long Candles

Short Candles

A *short candle* (Fig. 3-5), or short day, shows indecision among buyers and sellers as the price ended the day very close to where it began. Short candles derive their significance based on where they appear. For example, a short candle in a sideways or choppy market merely reinforces the indecision that is already demonstrated by the choppy market activity. Conversely, a short candle in a trending market has great meaning as buyers and sellers struggled for control of price direction. That signifies that a change in price direction may be imminent. Volume is also used to determine the significance of a short candle. Short candles that form on higher than normal volume in trending markets show that sellers are stepping up their activity in an uptrend, or that buyers are stepping up their activity in a downtrend. Think of a short candle on higher volume as the trend hitting a brick wall. Sometimes price will continue and break through that wall, but in many cases, a price reversal of some sort follows the short candle. No matter how compelling a short candle looks as a trend reversal point, it is still not wise to place a trade without some form of confirmation that a price reversal is indeed taking place.

The color of the candle is not as important as the close proximity of the opening and closing price, especially in trending markets.

FIGURE 3-5 • Short Candles

Marubozu

Candles can also be classified into groups based on whether or not shadows are present. The lack of a shadow at either end shows strong conviction among either buyers or sellers depending on the type of candle and on which end the shadow is missing. For example, the lack of an upper shadow on a long white candle shows that enough buying pressure was exerted for price to close at that day's high price, which is a bullish indication.

A candle that has no upper shadow is referred to as a *shaven head*, while a candle that has no lower shadow is referred to as a *shaven bottom*. The Japanese term for these situations is *marubozu*, which means "bald or shaven head."

A *white marubozu* is the term given to a white candle that has no shadow at either end. This is bullish as price opened at its low for the day and closed at its high for the day, demonstrating that buyers were in control throughout the entire session.

A *black marubozu* is the term given to a black candle that has no shadow at either end. This is a bearish candle as it shows that price opened at its high for the day and closed at its low for the day, showing that sellers were in control throughout the session.

An *opening marubozu* is a candle that has no shadow at the opening price end of the candle. For example, a white candle would have no lower shadow or a black candle would have no upper shadow.

A *closing marubozu* is a candle that has no shadow at the closing price end of the candle. In this case, that would mean that a white candle would have no upper shadow or that a black candle would have no lower shadow.

Marubozu lines (Fig. 3-6) have more meaning if they appear on long candles. Since short candles typically represent trader indecision, the lack of an upper or lower shadow does not have the same implications as the lack of a shadow on a long candle. For instance, the lack of a lower shadow on a long white candle means that price opened at its low for the day and never looked back. This is bullish and is the basis for the belt hold line reversal pattern that will be discussed in Chapter 4.

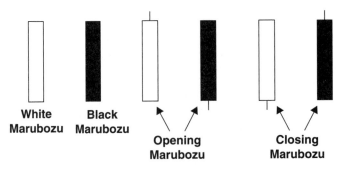

FIGURE 3-6 • Marubozu Lines

 Still Struggling

This new terminology is helpful in understanding candlesticks.

It is good to learn this terminology if you want to effectively communicate with other technicians about what you see in the market. Following are the main questions to remember.

- Is a trend in place?
- Is the candle white or black?
- Is the real body long or short?
- Are shadows present at either or both ends? If so, how long are they?

Answering these questions can help you get a quicker read on the psychology of traders as market trends unfold. It will take practice to get comfortable using candlesticks if you are used to other charting methods, but stick with it and you will see that candlesticks offer much more than ordinary bar or line charts.

Spinning Top

A *spinning top* (Fig. 3-7) is a candle that has a small or short real body with shadows at each end. In order to be classified as a spinning top, the shadows at each end should be at least twice as long as the real body. This shows that buyers and sellers each temporarily had the upper hand during the session, but in the end, price closed close to where it opened. This shows classic indecision among traders as they failed to reach a consensus on price direction for the day. This is especially meaningful in a trending market. The appearance of a spinning top in a trending market is an indication that a change in price direction may be imminent. The classic definition of a spinning top aside, the mere presence of a short real body in a trending market is enough evidence to me that a change may be taking place, especially on heavier than normal volume. It is always important to not get so caught up in the classic definition of a candle line that obvious implications by a candle's appearance are overlooked.

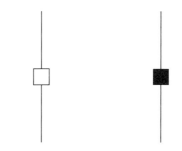

**The color of the candle is not important.
The candle itself shows indecision as bulls
and bears battle for control.**

FIGURE 3-7 • Spinning Tops

Doji

A *doji* (Fig. 3-8) is a very important candle line in candlestick analysis as it shows that neither buyers nor sellers were able to gain the upper hand by the end of the day as the opening and closing prices were virtually equal. Just like the spinning top, a doji that appears in a trending market has more significance than a doji that appears in a range bound, choppy market. Another important point is that a doji gains more importance if there are very few doji in the candles preceding it.

$$+$$

**A doji shows indecision among traders as the open
and close for the period are very close, if not identical.**

FIGURE 3-8 • Doji

A doji's predictive ability seems to be more reliable in an up-trending market than a down-trending market simply because of the psychology in each situation. The trader mindset in an uptrend is much more sanguine than in that of a downtrend. Also, some form of demand or buying pressure is needed to push prices higher. The appearance of a doji in an uptrend can be a signal that the buying pressure necessary to continue the uptrend may be waning, or that selling pressure may be increasing. In many cases a doji in a downtrend will not yield a reversal since price can continue to fall "under its own weight" with the absence of buying pressure to stabilize prices.

Doji Types

Although a doji is classified as such by the close proximity of its opening and closing prices, there are three other classifications of doji that represent different aspects of trader psychology. The location of the opening and closing prices in the daily trading range along with the length and location of shadows can help a trader identify specific doji lines.

A *long-legged doji* (Fig. 3-9) is identified by long upper and lower shadows, which signify an intense battle between buyers and sellers. During the day, each side appeared to be winning the battle as long shadows were formed. In the end, however, the day ends in a stalemate since the opening and closing prices are virtually equal. The location of the opening and closing prices should be at or near the center of the candle. Of course, many long-legged doji will not be symmetrical with equal length upper and lower shadows. The key here is to look for long shadows in relation to the other candles preceding it. This is an especially strong signal in a trending market as it shows that countertrend forces were able to halt the advance or decline, depending on the direction of the trend

A *gravestone doji* (Fig. 3-10) has bearish implications in an uptrend as it shows that the opening and closing prices were at the bottom of the daily range. Its name is derived from soldiers dying in battle, which equates to the end of an uptrend. This could also be a reference to late buyers. This variety of doji shows that price was pushed sharply upward after the open, which showed tremendous buyer interest. That buying, however, was met with selling force

A long-legged doji shows a battle over price direction that ends in a stalemate for the period.

FIGURE 3-9 • Long-Legged Doji

A gravestone doji is bearish as it shows the inability of buyers to sustain upward price movement.

FIGURE 3-10 • Gravestone Doji

that was sufficient to push the closing price back down to the open. A day that started with much promise is now nothing more than a stalemate between buyers and sellers. Believe it or not, the appearance of a gravestone doji in a downtrend can actually have bullish implications because it attracts late, weak short sellers who can provide fuel for an advance if they are forced to cover their positions. Great care must be taken before trading this doji in a downtrend, however.

A *dragonfly doji* (Fig. 3-11) has bullish implications when it appears in a downtrend. It is the opposite of the gravestone doji in that price opens at its high for the day before sellers push the price sharply lower. As the trading day develops, however, there is a strong push among buyers to force price back up to where it opened. Just when it seemed that sellers were ready to continue the downtrend in a strong way, the price reversed, which attracted more buyers. The name *dragonfly doji* symbolizes a dragonfly spreading its wings to take flight. Again, however, this doji has opposite implications in an uptrend. Its appearance can be a bearish sign as it shows that sellers have become more active as demonstrated by the long lower shadow. The long lower shadow in this case is evidence of a weakening uptrend.

A dragonfly doji is bullish in downtrends as it shows the inability of sellers to sustain downward price movement.

FIGURE 3-11 • Dragonfly Doji

Stars

A *star* (Fig. 3-12) is a candle that has strong reversal implications in a trending market. The psychology behind this pattern shows that the trend in force is in danger of reversing. A star reversal pattern consists of multiple candles that are classified into four varieties, which will be covered in Chapter 4.

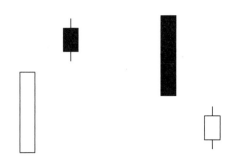

The formation of a star in a trending market is a sign that the prevailing trend may be in danger of reversing.

FIGURE 3-12 • Stars

A star is formed when a small bodied candle gaps away from the real body of the previous candle. It is preferred, but not necessary, for the real body of the star to form outside the shadow of the previous day. Stars commonly occur as either a spinning top or doji. The gap is in the direction of the trend, which means an upside gap in an uptrend or a downside gap in a downtrend. The reversal implication is stronger if one forms following either a long white candle in an uptrend or a long black candle in a downtrend. The color of the real body of the candle that forms the star is not nearly as important as the mere presence of a small bodied candle in a trending market. The fact that the candle gaps in the direction of the trend followed by a small real body shows that whatever early emotion was shown by traders following the strong trending action of the previous day could not be sustained. There are different classifications of stars such as *morning star* and *evening star*, which will be discussed in Chapter 4.

Umbrella Lines

Umbrella lines (Fig. 3-13) are single candle lines that also have strong reversal implications. These lines resemble the dragonfly doji; the only difference is the small real body as opposed to the doji where the opening and closing prices are virtually equal. Umbrella lines are labeled as such because their appearance resembles that of an umbrella with a long handle, or a "paper umbrella" in the original Japanese literature. Two umbrella lines called the hammer and hanging man will be discussed in Chapter 4. Just like the doji, these lines gain their significance from where they appear in a trending market.

FIGURE 3-13 • Umbrella Lines

Summary

- Basic candlestick lines form the foundation for more complex patterns.
- The real body represents the difference between the opening and closing prices for the day.
- Shadows connect the real body to the extreme high and low prices for the day.
- Long candles show strong conviction among traders based on the color.
- Short candles show indecision as the opening and closing prices are close together.
- Marubozu lines are formed by the absence of shadows on either or both ends of a candle.
- Marubozu are more meaningful on long candles.

- Spinning tops show indecision and a potential reversal in trending markets as buyers and sellers were unable to reach a consensus on price direction.
- Doji are likely reversal signals in trending markets as buyers and sellers battled to a virtual stalemate.
- Stars are small bodied candles that form in the direction of the trend by gapping away from the real body of the previous candle but finish the day with little price movement.
- Umbrella lines are close relatives of the dragonfly doji and have strong reversal implications depending on their appearance in a trending market.

QUIZ

1. **Candlesticks highlight the difference between the opening and closing prices.**
   A. True
   B. False

2. **Shadows represent**
   A. The difference between the opening and closing prices
   B. The time of day that a trade was made
   C. The extreme high and/or low price of the day
   D. None of the above

3. **A small real body represents**
   A. Trader indecision
   B. Strong trader conviction
   C. A guaranteed reversal in price direction
   D. Both A and C

4. **A spinning top is most meaningful in**
   A. A trending market regardless of direction
   B. A sideways or choppy market
   C. Only in uptrends
   D. Only in downtrends

5. **Doji are labeled as such because**
   A. The high price virtually matches the previous day's high price
   B. The candle has long shadow(s)
   C. The opening and closing prices are very far apart
   D. The opening and closing prices are virtually equal

6. **Marubozu are classified by**
   A. The absence of an upper shadow
   B. The absence of a lower shadow
   C. The absence of a shadow at either end
   D. All of the above

7. **A dragonfly doji has**
   A. A long upper shadow
   B. Long shadows at both ends
   C. A long lower shadow
   D. None of the above

8. **A star is most meaningful when it appears**
   A. In a trending market
   B. Following a long candle in the direction of the trend
   C. In a choppy market
   D. Both A and B

9. **Which doji has a long upper shadow and a long lower shadow?**
   A. Gravestone doji
   B. Dragonfly doji
   C. Long-legged doji
   D. Shaven head doji

10. **The color of a short candle is not as important as the formation of the short candle itself.**
    A. True
    B. False

Chapter **4**

Candlestick Reversal Patterns

Candlestick reversal patterns capture the very essence of the candlestick charting methodology. Knowing when trader psychology is changing is paramount to either locking in a trading profit or entering a new position as price changes direction.

CHAPTER OBJECTIVES

In this chapter, you will

- Learn when a reversal pattern is valid
- Identify strong reversal patterns that demand immediate action
- See more subtle, longer term patterns that take time to develop
- Learn how to confirm reversal patterns
- Understand reversal pattern trading examples

Remember that the goal of technical analysis is to gather enough pieces of evidence to determine what price is *likely* to do. By the time you finish with this book, you will know what those pieces are and how to assemble them. This chapter addresses the very important piece of candlestick reversal patterns. Consider these reversal patterns to be the basic building blocks that when combined with other indicators can help traders identify high percentage trading opportunities.

These reversal patterns reflect a short-term change in trader psychology that can lead to opportunities for profit. One of the most basic points to remember is that in order for a reversal pattern to be labeled as such, there must be a trend to reverse. In other words, if any of these patterns show up in a choppy, trendless market, the meaning is greatly diminished. Also, it is important to note that some of these patterns are meaningful only in uptrends or downtrends. For example, a piercing line is a bullish reversal pattern. If a piercing line is formed in an uptrend, it is not a reversal pattern. Keep that in mind as you learn these patterns.

This chapter begins with the reversal patterns that give the strongest signals and will progress to those that either take more time to develop or are more subtle in their development. The most common and simplest reversal patterns used today will be covered. Every example will discuss the psychology behind each pattern along with trading tips and stop order placement for risk control. One final note—the appearance of these patterns does not guarantee a trend reversal. These patterns only alert a trader that the psychology in the market is such that the odds of a reversal have increased. Always wait for price to confirm the reversal before entering a trade. This means that waiting for the closing price to confirm the reversal is preferred, but more aggressive traders may want to enter a position when price trades above or below the confirmation level, depending on the trend. No matter which camp you are in (aggressive or conservative), always use protective stop loss orders on every trade.

Strong Signal Patterns

These reversal patterns are labeled as such because their appearance demands immediate attention as they show a rather abrupt change in trader sentiment. The patterns presented in this section are the hammer, hanging man, engulfing pattern, piercing line, dark cloud cover, and stars.

Hammer and Hanging Man

The *hammer* and *hanging man* patterns (Fig. 4-1) are umbrella lines that get their meanings from the context in which they appear. The two candles are identical in their identifying characteristics; their name and implications depend on the direction of the trend. These examples show the candles with no upper shadow, but a small upper shadow is permissible.

Hammer

The hammer forms in a down-trending market and is an indication buyers are stepping up, which means a bottom may be near. It gets its name because it is a short body with a long lower shadow resembling the shape of a hammer. This candle also provides early evidence that the market may be trying to "hammer out" a bottom.

**The hammer and hanging man look the same. Their
names and meaning are derived from the context in
which they appear. The real body color is not important.**

FIGURE 4-1 • Hammer and Hanging Man

The daily chart of Baidu Inc. (Fig. 4-2) shows an example of a hammer. Notice that the candles preceding the hammer were mostly black with shorter lower shadows. That showed sellers were driving the price lower with the daily closes fairly close to the low price of the day. The appearance of the hammer formed the longest lower shadow in weeks, an indication of buying activity. The fact that the closing price was so close to the opening price (as demonstrated by the small real body) indicated that buyers had turned what looked to be a continuation of the downtrend into a stalemate for the day.

FIGURE 4-2 • Hammer: Baidu Inc., Daily

Source: MetaStock

The psychology behind the pattern is relatively simple to see.

- Price has to be in a downtrend or moving lower.
- Trade opens and sellers apply pressure, pushing price considerably lower.
- Buyers appear and push price back up to near where it opened.
- This means that a day that had clearly favored the sellers ended in a stalemate that encourages new buyers.

Notice that after the hammer formed, it still took almost two weeks for price to begin to move significantly higher. This illustrates that while the formation of a hammer is a bullish event, it may still take some time for buyers to be able to assert themselves enough to actually change the trend. This means that there is no reason to recklessly enter a buy trade just because a hammer forms. Always wait for price to trade above the high of the hammer before initiating a new position. A protective stop loss order should be placed just below the low of the hammer.

Hanging Man

The hanging man forms in an up-trending market and is an indication that sellers are increasing their activity. This pattern gets its name because the small real body and long lower shadow resemble a man who is hanging. While price fought its way back up close to where it opened, this still has bearish implications because it is a small real body in a trending market, which shows trader indecision.

The daily chart of Texas Instruments Inc. (Fig. 4-3) shows an example of the hanging man. Notice that price gapped higher on the day of the hanging man before sellers emerged to produce the long lower shadow. Buyers increased their activity later in the session to push the closing price very close to where it opened, resulting in a stalemate for the day. A day that had started with so much promise in the direction of the trend ended up being disheartening for those holding shares.

There are four keys to the psychology behind this pattern.

1. Price has to be in an uptrend and moving higher.
2. Trade opens and sellers apply pressure, pushing prices lower.
3. Buyers appear and push price back up to near where it opened.
4. A day that had opened with so much promise on the gap higher open ended in disappointment as there was little upside progress made after the open.

This particular hanging man pattern precipitated a rather sharp, sudden decline. This is a pattern that can be used by those holding shares to simply exit

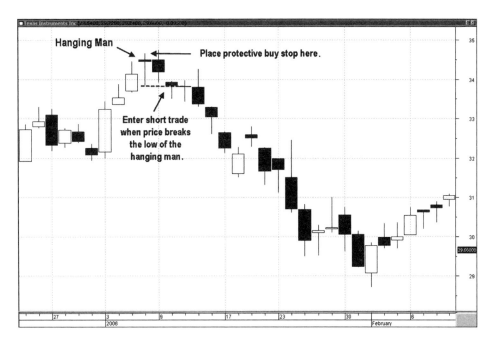

FIGURE 4-3 • Hanging Man: Texas Instruments Inc., Daily
Source: MetaStock

positions on a break of the low of the hanging man, or to enter a short position for more aggressive traders. Those that enter short positions on these patterns need to remember to place a protective stop loss just above the high of the hanging man.

While the hammer and hanging man patterns stand out as indications that the activity of countertrend forces are beginning to increase, it is always wise to wait for some form of confirmation that a reversal is taking place. *This means that single candle patterns should never be traded unless price actually does reverse.* Also be aware that the longer the tail on either candle, the more risk for the trader as the stop loss price will be that much further away from the trade entry price.

Engulfing Pattern

An *engulfing pattern* (Fig. 4-4) is a strong two-candle reversal pattern that forms when a candle completely engulfs the real body of the preceding candle of the opposite color. Remember that in order for this to be a valid reversal pattern, there must be a price trend in force to reverse. This pattern is similar to the outside day reversal pattern used in Western technical analysis. The main difference is that the outside day requires the entire previous candle to be contained by the reversal candle, while the engulfing pattern only compares real

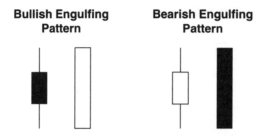

Bullish Engulfing Pattern

Bearish Engulfing Pattern

Whether or not the candles have tails or shadows is irrelevant. An engulfing pattern is measured only by the length of the real bodies.

FIGURE 4-4 • Engulfing Patterns

bodies or the range between the opening and closing prices. Even though only real bodies are considered when classifying an engulfing pattern, as more of the previous candle is engulfed by the real body of the current candle, the signal becomes stronger.

A *bullish engulfing* pattern occurs in a downtrend and consists of a black candle followed by a white candle whose real body engulfs the black real body of the previous day's black candle. This pattern starts with a move lower in a downtrend as evidenced by a black candle. The following day, price gaps away from the previous day's close in the direction of the trend before reversing higher and closing above the previous black candle's open. This, in effect, wipes out the entire previous day's losses and turns these two trading days into a positive return when these candles are combined. In this case, when the two candles that make up a bullish engulfing pattern are combined (Fig. 4-5), the end result is a candle that resembles a hammer, which is itself a bullish reversal candle.

The bullish engulfing pattern forms a bullish candle when the two are combined.

FIGURE 4-5 • Bullish Engulfing Pattern Combined

The daily chart of Freeport McMoRan Copper and Gold Inc. (Fig. 4-6) shows an example of a bullish engulfing pattern. When one steps through the

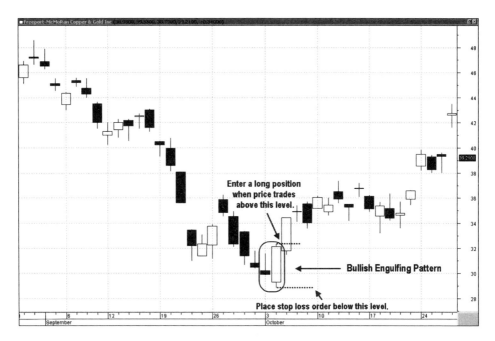

FIGURE 4-6 Bullish Engulfing Pattern: Freeport McMoRan Copper and Gold Inc., Daily
Source: MetaStock

psychology behind the pattern, it is easy to see why this reversal pattern is viewed as a bullish event.

1. The price trend is down as evidenced by declining prices on the left side of the chart.
2. On the first day of the engulfing pattern, buyers try to get something going but fail as evidenced by the long upper shadow.
3. On the second day of the pattern, price gaps lower at the open, embolding sellers.
4. Price then reverses higher and closes much higher for the day, an obvious win for buyers.
5. In fact, the second day's real body completely engulfs the *entire* previous day's candle.

Patterns such as this reinforce the actions by new buyers as evidence that market psychology has reversed, at least for the short term. No doubt some of the early buying action is helped by weak shorts covering their positions as price begins to reverse, but this is a clear win for the buyers.

When trading this pattern, it is best to enter a long position when price moves above the high of the engulfing candle, or the long white candle formed on the second day of the pattern. This provides confirmation that the trend has indeed reversed. For risk control, a stop loss order should be placed below the lowest point of the pattern, whether it is the low of the first day or the low of the second day. In this case, the stop loss order should have been placed below the low of the second day's candle.

A *bearish engulfing pattern* forms in an up-trending market and consists of a white candle followed by a black candle that completely engulfs the real body of the previous white candle. The psychology is the same as the bullish engulfing pattern, only in the opposite direction. Again, when the two candles are combined, the result is a bearish-looking candle.

The bearish engulfing pattern forms a bearish candle when the two are combined.

FIGURE 4-7 • Bearish Engulfing Pattern Combined

The daily chart of the Guggenheim Solar ETF (Fig. 4-8) shows an example of a bearish engulfing pattern. Look for five pieces to the breakdown of the reversal.

1. The price trend is higher as evidenced by the rising prices on the left side of the chart.
2. On the first day of the pattern, a white candle forms, showing that buyers are in control.
3. On the second day price gaps higher and then reverses lower as sellers became much more active.
4. Price reverses and closes sharply lower on the day, a win for the sellers.
5. The second day's candle completely engulfs the first, showing a sharp change in psychology.

There are two ways to play this pattern. First, more conservative long only traders can simply exit their long positions when the lowest point of the two-candle pattern is violated. Second, more aggressive traders who want to play the short side can place short trades once the lowest point of the two-candle pattern is violated. A protective buy stop should be placed above the highest point of the two-candle pattern.

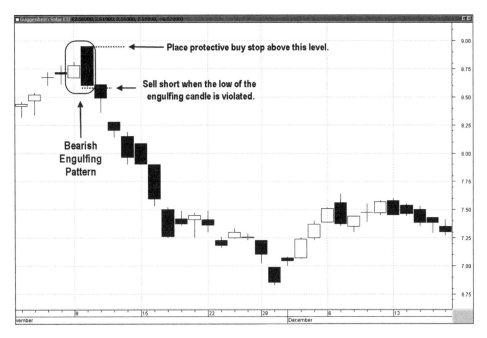

FIGURE 4-8 • Bearish Engulfing Pattern: Guggenheim Solar ETF, Daily

Source: MetaStock

Piercing Line

The *piercing line* (Fig. 4-9) is a two-candle reversal pattern that occurs in downtrends. Just like the bullish engulfing pattern, the first day is a candle that moves in the direction of the downtrend (in this case a dark candle). However, the second day begins in favor of the bears as that day's opening price gaps below the low point of the previous day's candle. Notice that the gap is below the low point on the *entire* previous day's candle including the lower shadow,

**The second candle opens below the low of the first
candle, then reverses higher and closes at least
halfway into the real body of the first candle.**

FIGURE 4-9 • Piercing Line

not just the real body. The pattern is completed on the second day when the white candle closes at least halfway into the real body of the previous day's black candle.

A closer look at the two-day pattern shows that when the days are combined into one candle, the result is a bullish-looking hammer. Even though the real body of the hammer is black in this case, it is important to remember that the combination of the two candles yields a small bodied candle with a long lower shadow—a classic reversal pattern.

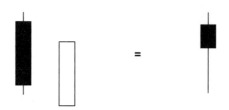

A bullish looking hammer is formed when the two days of the piercing line pattern are combined.

FIGURE 4-10 • Piercing Line Combined

The daily chart of Titanium Metals Corp. (Fig. 4-11) shows an example of a piercing line reversal pattern. Let's step through the psychology behind this pattern.

1. Price is in a downtrend as evidenced by the falling prices into the October low.
2. The first day of the pattern is a longer black candle, which closes very near its low price.
3. The second day price opens sharply lower, gapping below the low of the previous day's candle.
4. Price then reverses higher, closing above the midpoint of the first day's black candle.

The message in this pattern is bullish. The first day a long black candle that closes near its low for the day is a clear win for the bears. The second day price gaps below the low of the first day, getting the bears even more excited, which attracts late short players as they sense a continued breakdown in the trend. Price then rebounds and closes more than halfway into the real body of the previous candle, which reverses early weakness. This is a clear win for the bulls.

When trading this pattern, a protective sell stop should be placed below the low of the second candle.

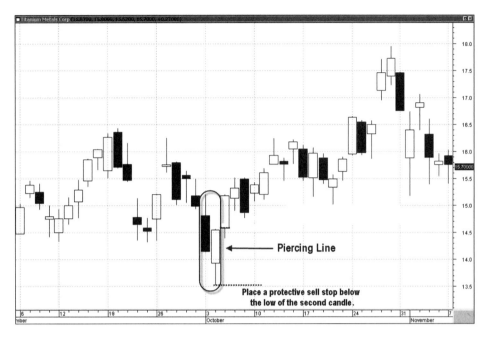

FIGURE 4-11 • Piercing Line: Titanium Metals Corp., Daily
Source: MetaStock

Dark Cloud Cover

A *dark cloud cover* (Fig. 4-12) is the bearish counterpart of the piercing line. This pattern forms in an uptrend and turns what begins as a bullish event into a strong bearish reversal signal. The first day consists of a long white candle that moves in the direction of the trend, followed by a candle that gaps completely above the high of the white candle before reversing lower to close at least halfway into the real body of the first day's candle.

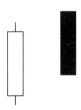

**The second candle opens over the high of the
white candle and then reverses and closes at least
halfway into the white candle's real body.**

FIGURE 4-12 • Dark Cloud Cover

When the two days of the pattern are combined into a single candle (Fig. 4-13), the bearish message is evident. After pushing to new highs during the pattern, price reverses and closes lower, forming a small bodied candle with a long upper shadow. This is an inverted hammer, which will be covered later in this chapter with star reversal patterns.

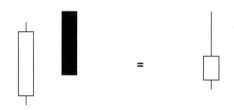

The dark cloud cover forms a bearish inverted hammer when the two candles are combined.

FIGURE 4-13 • Dark Cloud Cover Combined

The daily chart of NVIDIA Corp. (Fig. 4-14) shows an example of a dark cloud cover. The pattern develops in four steps.

1. Price is in an uptrend as evidenced by the rising prices on the left side of the chart.
2. On the first day of the pattern, a long white candle forms, confirming the uptrend.
3. On the next day, price gaps above the high of the white candle before reversing lower.
4. Price closes at least halfway into the real body of the previous day's white candle.

The psychology of this pattern is bearish as the first day confirms the uptrend, which is comforting to the bulls. The second day opens with some euphoria as price gaps above the high (upper shadow) of the white candle before reversing lower. This creates doubt among the bulls as to the sustainability of the upward move. This causes nervous bulls to exit, which builds downside momentum. When trading this pattern a protective buy stop should be placed above the high of the black candle.

One important point to remember regarding these two patterns is the more they close into the real body of the previous day's candle, the stronger the signal. If the reversal moves past the other extreme of the previous day's real body, an engulfing pattern is formed, which is an even stronger reversal signal than the piercing line or dark cloud cover.

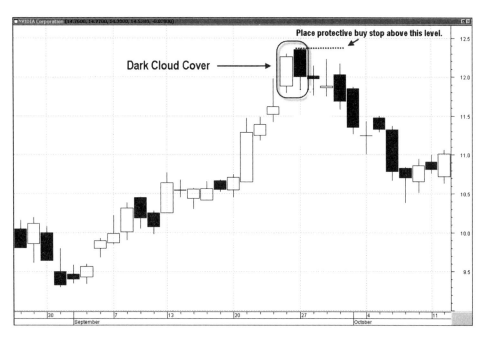

FIGURE 4-14 • Dark Cloud Cover: NVIDIA Corp., Daily
Source: MetaStock

Stars

Stars are single small bodied candles that gap away from the prior candle's real body in the direction of the trend. Their appearance can signify that the trend is in danger of reversing, or pausing at the very least. Remember that while stars are powerful signals that a reversal may be imminent, there is no way of knowing how sharp the reversal will be or how far it will go. The key to successful trading of these patterns is waiting for price confirmation of a change in direction and then acting quickly when placing a trade. Star reversal patterns come in four varieties—morning star, evening star, doji star, and shooting star. In each case, it is permissible for the star's real body to overlap the shadow of its preceding candle, but the real bodies cannot come in contact with each other. A gap between the second and third candles of each pattern is preferred but not necessary.

Morning Star

A *morning star* pattern (Fig. 4-15) occurs in a downtrend and is a sign that the downtrend may be ready to reverse. As its name implies, it stands for a sunrise, or hope that price will begin to move higher.

The pattern consists of three candles. The first candle is a long black candle that reinforces the downtrend in price. The second candle gaps away from the

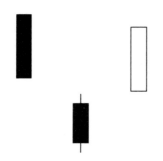

**The color of the real body on the
second candle is unimportant.**

FIGURE 4-15 • Morning Star

previous day's black candle and forms a small real body, which shows little price movement after the gap lower. The color of the real body on the second candle is not as important as the fact that a small real body candle has formed in a downtrend, which shows more equilibrium in buying and selling pressure. The third candle trades higher following the small real body of the second candle and ends higher on the day, forming a white candle that penetrates the real body of the first candle in the pattern. A gap between the second candle and third candle is not necessary; if a gap is present, however, it is considered an even stronger signal.

The daily chart of Citigroup Inc. (Figure 4-16) shows an example of a morning star pattern. While this is not a classic example of a morning star reversal in that the day preceding the morning star is not a long black candle, the implications are the same.

1. Price is in a downtrend.
2. The first of the three candles is a black candle that gaps lower, reinforcing the downtrend.
3. The second candle gaps substantially lower, which encourages the bears even more.
4. Price makes no further downward progress after the open as a small white candle forms.
5. Price gaps higher and continues higher on the third day as buyers complete the reversal.

An increase in volume on the third candle shows an increase in buyer conviction and helps confirm the reversal. When trading this pattern, a close above the real body of the star candle is confirmation that a reversal is under way. A protective sell stop should be placed below the low of the second candle.

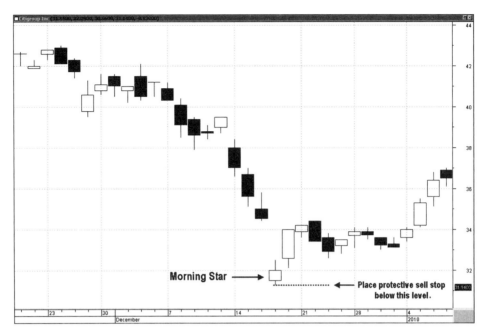

FIGURE 4-16 • Morning Star: Citigroup Inc., Daily

Source: MetaStock

Evening Star

As the name implies, the *evening star* pattern is a warning of a dark period for prices as the sun may be setting on a rally phase. This is also a three-candle pattern that unfolds in an uptrend. The stronger the trend, the stronger is the reversal implication.

The first candle is typically a long white candle that reinforces the strength of the uptrend. The second candle gaps away from the real body of the long white candle but forms a small body that signifies a struggle between buyers

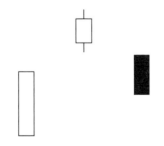

The color of the real body on the second candle is unimportant.

FIGURE 4-17 • Evening Star

and sellers for price direction. This is an indication that buying interest is lessening or selling interest is gaining strength, or both. The third day consists of a black candle that penetrates into the real body of the first candle of the pattern (the long white candle preceding the star). Just as with the morning star pattern, a gap between the second candle and third candle is not necessary, but if one does form, it gives a stronger reversal signal.

The daily chart of Intel Corp. (Fig. 4-18) shows an example of an evening star pattern. There are give steps in this sequence.

1. Price is in an uptrend.
2. The first candle is a long white candle that forms as price tries to break into new high ground.
3. The second candle gaps away from the first, which encourages the bulls.
4. All that can be mustered on that day, however, is a small bodied white candle.
5. Price gaps lower on the third day, demoralizing the bulls and completing the reversal.

An increase in volume on the third candle shows increasing trader conviction and helps confirm the reversal. When trading this pattern, a protective buy stop should be placed over the high of the second (or star) candle.

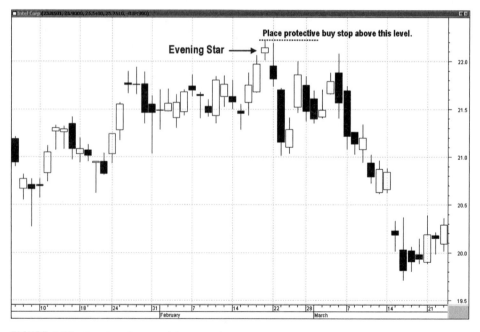

FIGURE 4-18 • Evening Star: Intel Corp., Daily
Source: MetaStock

Doji Star

A *doji star* reversal (Figure 4-19) is as the name implies—the star candle is actually a doji. This is a very strong reversal pattern as it demonstrates that the gap move in the direction of the trend on the star candle saw no continued movement whatsoever in that direction at the close. Doji star reversal patterns come in two varieties, the doji morning star and the doji evening star. Since the morning and evening star patterns have been covered, we will only show an example of a doji star here.

The key to the doji star pattern is the gap between the real bodies between the first and second candles.

FIGURE 4-19 • Doji Stars

The daily chart of Guggenheim Solar ETF shows an example of a morning doji star reversal. This was a particularly strong signal because price was in a strong downtrend heading into the reversal. There are five pieces to the psychology behind the pattern.

1. Price is in a strong downtrend.
2. The first candle of the pattern is black and gaps lower, reinforcing the strength of the trend.
3. Price gaps lower on the second (doji) day, giving the bears more confidence.
4. Price fails to make any downside headway whatsoever, showing a change in sentiment.
5. Price gaps sharply higher on the third day, forcing late short sellers to cover positions.

As with the other star reversal patterns, a protective sell stop should have been placed below the low of the doji.

With regard to doji star reversals, if there is complete separation between the candles (no overlap of any kind), these doji reversal patterns are referred to in Japanese literature as *abandoned babies*. A morning doji star that has no overlap of any kind with the other two candles (shadows included) is referred to as an

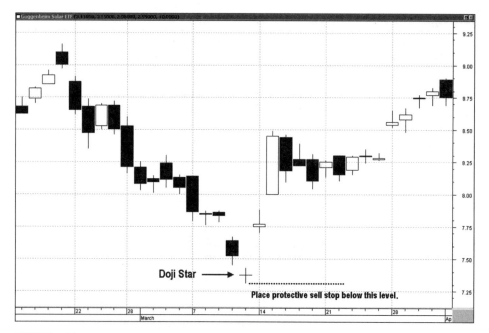

FIGURE 4-20 • Doji Morning Star: Guggenheim Solar ETF, Daily
Source: MetaStock

abandoned baby bottom. An evening doji star that has no overlap is referred to as an *abandoned baby top.* These are very rare, yet very powerful reversal signals. In fact, the morning doji star example (Fig. 4-20) is a great example of an abandoned baby bottom.

Shooting Star or Inverted Hammer

The *shooting star* (Fig. 4-21) and inverted hammer are presented together because the candle that forms each one is identical. The difference between them is the context in which they appear. A shooting star is a sign of a reversal in an uptrend and has to have that distinguishing star quality—its real body must gap away from the real body of the previous candle.

A shooting stars consists of a small real body and a long upper shadow. The color of the real body is unimportant.

FIGURE 4-21 • Shooting Star

FIGURE 4-22 • Shooting Star: Arch Coal Inc., Daily
Source: MetaStock

The shooting star is a pattern that once again shows continuation of a strong uptrend by gapping higher at the open and moving higher during the trading day. During the day, however, the tide turns and sellers push the price back down near where it opened, showing an increase in selling activity. The longer the upper shadow, the stronger is the reversal implication. The daily chart of Arch Coal Inc. (Fig. 4-22) shows an example of the shooting star reversal pattern.

1. Price is in an uptrend.
2. A long white candle forms, reinforcing the strength of the uptrend.
3. Price forms a slight gap higher and continues on before sellers push the price back down.
4. The long upper shadow demoralizes the bulls.
5. Price reverses lower on the third day, completing the reversal.

If the real body of the shooting star candle forms a doji, the result would be a bearish gravestone doji—a very strong reversal signal. When trading the shooting star pattern, place a protective buy stop above the high of the second (or shooting star) candle.

The inverted hammer looks identical to the shooting star but has reversal implications in downtrends. Believe it or not, a candle such as this appearing in a downtrend can actually make short sellers overconfident as price tries to rally

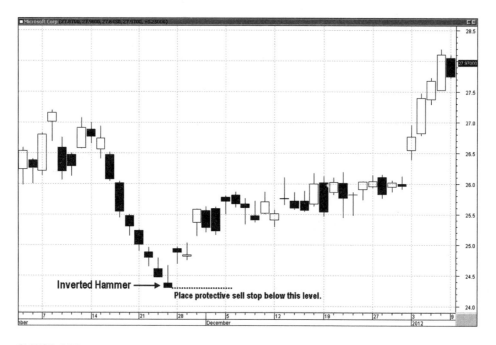

FIGURE 4-23 • Inverted Hammer: Microsoft Corp., Daily
Source: MetaStock

but fails intra-day. The key here, however, is the formation of a long upper shadow, which signifies that buyers were active during the session, even though they were not able to hold gains. The following day, in some cases, may start out trading lower before buyers become active again, this time forcing those that added late short positions to cover, forcing prices higher.

The daily chart of Microsoft Corp. (Fig. 4-23) shows an example of an inverted hammer. When looking at this pattern, notice the long upper shadow on the inverted hammer candle, which had a longer upper shadow than the previous six candles during the decline.

1. Price is in a strong downtrend.
2. On the inverted hammer day, price gaps lower before reversing and trading higher.
3. Sellers force the closing price back below the opening price, giving comfort to the bears.
4. The long upper shadow is evidence of increased buying activity, however.
5. The following day price reverses higher, forcing late shorts to cover.

When trading this pattern, a protective sell stop should be placed below the low of the inverted hammer.

This concludes the section on the stronger reversal patterns. Next are patterns that may not demand as much immediate attention but are important nonetheless.

Still Struggling

Reversal patterns are identified by the market conditions in which they appear.

Remember that each pattern gains its meaning from the context in which it appears. For example, the hammer and hanging man are essentially the same candle formation, but the hanging man shows developing weakness in an uptrend as sellers made a spirited effort during the trading day as demonstrated by the long lower shadow. That shows an increase in countertrend activity even if the bulls pushed the closing price back up near the open. The hammer, on the other hand, shows that sellers had their way early in the session as they pushed the price lower, only to have the bulls dig in their heels and begin buying shares to push the closing price back near the open. That activity shows that trader psychology may be changing and that the downtrend may be near an end. The piercing line and dark cloud cover are reciprocals of each other (dark cloud cover in an uptrend and the piercing line in a downtrend). The same goes for stars (evening star in an uptrend and morning star in a downtrend). In each case, just try to visualize the abrupt change in trader psychology represented by each pattern and you will begin to spot meaningful turning points in price movement.

More Subtle Patterns

There are more subtle patterns that do not demand immediate attention like the preceding group, but these patterns are still important as they may take more time to unfold or they may not show an immediate change in market sentiment like the stronger patterns just described.

Harami

A *harami* (Fig. 4-24) is a two-candle pattern that resembles the inside day in Western technical analysis. The difference between the two, however, is that the inside day requires the entire day's range to be inside the previous day, while the harami only compares the ranges of the real bodies. Think of the harami as a reverse engulfing pattern in which the real body of the second candle is

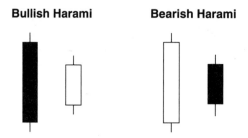

Bullish Harami   **Bearish Harami**

**The real body of the second candle must
be within the real body of the first.**

FIGURE 4-24 • Harami

engulfed by the real body of the first candle. In many cases, the color of the second candle is opposite the first, but that is not necessary to form a valid harami pattern. As with all of the other reversal patterns, the harami is only valid in a trending market. The term *harami* means "pregnant" in Japanese with the first candle representing the "mother" and the second, smaller candle representing the "baby."

The daily chart of BB&T Corp. (Fig. 4-25) shows an example of a bearish harami.

1. Price is moving higher as shown by consecutive white candles.
2. The first day of the pattern is a white candle that confirms the trend.
3. The second day price gaps lower at the open and forms a small black candle within the real body of the white candle.
4. Any meaningful decline on this day is muted by late longs seeing this as a buying opportunity.
5. A close below the low of the first candle is needed to confirm the reversal.

When trading a bearish harami, the trade should be entered on a close below the low of the first candle. A protective buy stop should be placed above the high of the first candle.

The daily chart of AFLAC Inc. (Fig. 4-26) shows an example of a bullish harami that develops in five steps.

1. Price is in a downtrend as demonstrated by consecutive black candles.
2. The first day of the pattern is a black candle that confirms the trend.
3. The second day price gaps higher at the open and forms a small white candle within the real body of the black candle.
4. Any meaningful advance on this day is muted by late shorts seeing this as a shorting opportunity.
5. A close above the high of the first candle is needed to confirm the reversal.

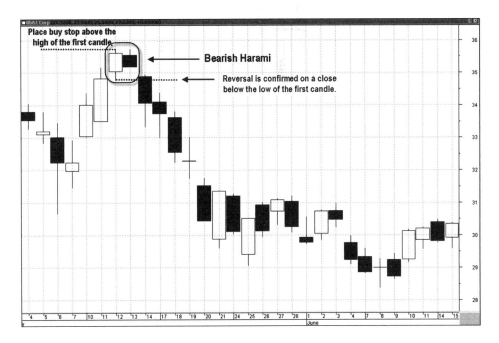

FIGURE 4-25 • Bearish Harami: BB&T Corp., Daily

Source: MetaStock

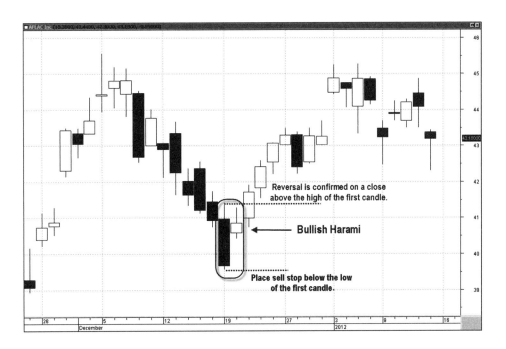

FIGURE 4-26 • Bullish Harami: AFLAC Inc., Daily

Source: MetaStock

FIGURE 4-27 • Harami Cross: Expedia Inc., Daily

Source: MetaStock

When trading a bullish harami, the trade should be entered on a close above the high of the first candle. A protective sell stop should be placed below the low of the first candle.

A *harami cross* employs the same psychology as the harami with the added strength of the second candle forming a doji. This is a very rare, yet powerful reversal pattern that still needs the same confirmation as the regular harami patterns. The daily chart of Expedia Inc. (Fig. 4-27) shows an example of a bullish harami cross. Notice how the real body on the second candle forms a doji, signifying that buyers and sellers reached a complete stalemate on the direction of price for that day. That is a very strong reversal signal in a trending market. The stronger the trend, the stronger is the reversal implication. Trade entry and stop placement are the same as the bullish harami example shown in Fig. 4-26.

Belt Hold Lines

Belt hold lines (Fig. 4-28) are single candle reversal patterns that occur in trending markets. They consist of either a long black candle in an uptrend or a long white candle in a downtrend. The appearance of a belt hold line signifies that countertrend forces are digging in their heels and trying to abruptly change price direction. The candle should have an opening marubozu, but a small shadow at the opening end is permissible. It is also important to note that belt hold lines are in many cases part of stronger reversal patterns such as piercing lines, dark cloud cover, or engulfing patterns.

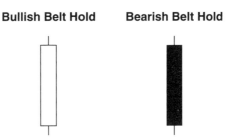

Bullish Belt Hold   **Bearish Belt Hold**

Belt hold lines can have small shadows at either end as long as the open and close are near the extremes for the period.

FIGURE 4-28 • Belt Hold Lines

A bullish belt hold occurs in a down-trending market. It is a long white candle that opens at or very near its low for the day. The bullish belt hold gains more importance if few belt hold candles have preceded it in the downtrend.

The daily chart of AK Steel Holding Corp. (Fig. 4-29) shows an example of a bullish belt hold line. Notice how price opened at the low of the day and reversed sharply higher as the belt hold line formed a bullish engulfing pattern with the preceding candle.

FIGURE 4-29 • Bullish Belt Hold: AK Steel Holding Corp., Daily

Source: MetaStock

FIGURE 4-30 • Bearish Belt Hold: Alcoa Inc., Daily
Source: MetaStock

A bearish belt hold occurs in an up-trending market. It is a long black candle that opens at or very near its high for the day. As with the bullish belt hold, the bearish belt hold gains more importance if few belt hold candles have preceded it in the uptrend.

The daily chart of Alcoa Inc. (Fig. 4-30) shows an example of a bearish belt hold. Price opened at its high of the day and traded sharply lower as the day progressed. This demonstrated that market psychology had shifted abruptly and that sellers were now in control.

It is not recommended that belt hold lines be traded on their own. Their importance is enhanced when they appear as part of one of the more powerful patterns mentioned previously (piercing line, dark cloud cover, or engulfing pattern).

Three White Soldiers

The *three white soldiers* pattern (Fig. 4-31) shows strength following either a market downtrend or a period of price consolidation. This pattern consists of three white candles closing progressively higher, giving the appearance of soldiers marching to higher levels.

Each day should open within the real body of the preceding day and then close at or near the high for the day. This demonstrates that sellers are winning the early battle as price gaps to a lower open, only to see buyers overwhelm their selling efforts as the day wears on, forcing a higher close. The key to this

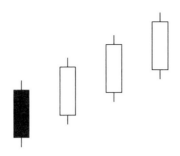

Each candle gaps into the real body of the previous candle and closes at or near the high of the period.

FIGURE 4-31 • Three White Soldiers

pattern is that each candle should form a white candle—but not too long a candle, otherwise price may be advancing too far too fast, which could cause profit taking or attract aggressive short sellers.

The daily chart of CONSOL Energy Inc. (Fig. 4-32) shows an example of three white soldiers. Notice how price reversed higher, and the three white candles marched steadily higher. The three advancing candles coming off of the low showed steady accumulation of shares by buyers, which causes prices to move higher.

FIGURE 4-32 • Three White Soldiers: CONSOL Energy Inc., Daily
Source: MetaStock

Be careful when trading this pattern as a three-day advance is likely to induce some profit taking. A three-day advance of this magnitude would also leave a trader in a rather unfavorable risk position with regard to the placement of a stop loss order, which should be under the low of the pattern. It would be prudent in this case to wait for a pullback of some sort before initiating a long position.

Three Black Crows

Three black crows (Fig. 4-33) is a three-day pattern that demonstrates the increasing strength of sellers following an uptrend. This pattern typically follows a long white candle in an uptrend and begins with a black candle opening within the body of the white candle and closing at or near its low for the day. The subsequent two days open within the real body of the previous black candle before moving lower, once again closing at or near the low of the day.

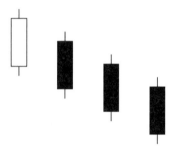

Each candle gaps into the real body of the previous candle and closes at or near the low of the period.

FIGURE 4-33 • Three Black Crows

The daily chart of Google Inc. (Fig. 4-34) actually shows two examples of the three black crows pattern. Notice in the first occurrence how the candles grow in length as the pattern progresses. This is an indication of increasing selling pressure that leads to the large price gap lower on the fourth black candle. The second occurrence also saw days two and three open within the real body of the preceding candle only to be overwhelmed by sellers who forced the price lower. In each case a period of price weakness followed. The Japanese expression "bad news has wings" definitely fits the appearance of this pattern.

As with the three white soldiers pattern, stop placement can be an issue when trading this pattern. Make sure you understand the amount of risk you are taking on with regard to trade entry versus the placement of your stop loss order.

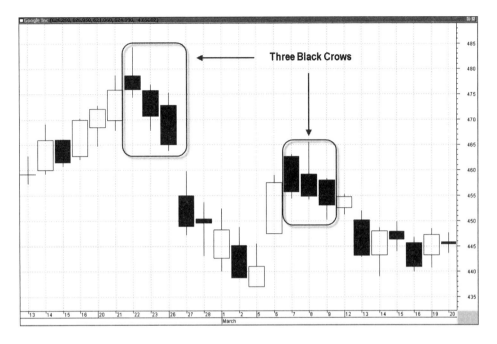

FIGURE 4-34 • Three Black Crows: Google Inc., Daily
Source: MetaStock

Meeting Lines

Meeting lines (Fig. 4-35), also known as *counterattack lines*, is a two-day pattern formed when two opposite colored candles come together and have matching (or very close) closing prices. This pattern is similar to the in-neck continuation pattern, discussed in Chapter 5.

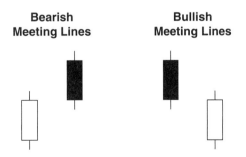

Meeting lines are identified by the second, opposite colored candle in the pattern. Black is bearish while white is bullish.

FIGURE 4-35 • Meeting Lines

The appearance of meeting lines shows that price movement in the direction of the trend has made a sudden stop. For example, on bullish meeting lines, sellers have their way the first day as evidenced by a long black candle. The second day gaps lower at the open, showing strong conviction among sellers. During the second day, however, buyers step up and force the closing price back to the same level as the prior day's black candle. The situation is reversed for bearish meeting lines as buyers have their way on the first day and beginning of the second day, only to see price reverse and close with no progress made with regard to the first day's close.

The term *counterattack lines* is sometimes used to name this pattern because countertrend forces "launch a counterattack" to stop the trend in its tracks. Another way of looking at these lines is to think that all good news has been "consumed" by the market in the bearish meeting lines because price gapped higher and traded lower the rest of the session. The same goes for bullish meeting lines in that long positions were disposed of by those wanting to exit as all discouraging news has been consumed by the market. The Japanese term for this pattern is *deaisen* or "lines that meet."

The daily chart of Cisco Systems Inc. (Fig. 4-36) shows an example of bearish meeting lines. There are four parts to the psychology behind the pattern.

1. Price is in an uptrend but in this case has taken a brief sideways pause.

2. The first day of the pattern is a white candle that encourages the bulls.

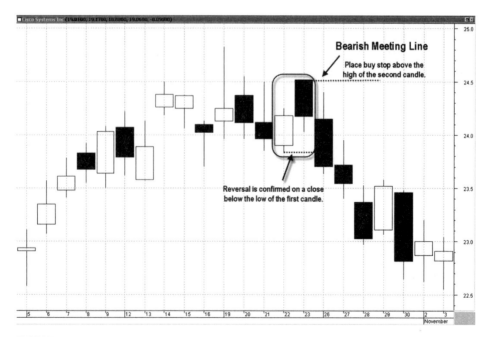

FIGURE 4-36 • Bearish Meeting Lines: Cisco Systems Inc., Daily
Source: MetaStock

3. The second day has a gap higher at the open, further encouraging the bulls.

4. Price sells off from the open, however, and ends with no gains from the prior day's close.

Look closely at Fig. 4-36 and notice that the bearish meeting lines pattern is actually an unfinished dark cloud cover since the closing price did not penetrate the real body of the previous candle. In the same way, the bullish meeting line is an unfinished piercing line. When trading this pattern, stop placement should be above the high of the second candle on the bearish meeting lines or below the low of the second candle of the bullish meeting lines.

Upside Gap Two Crows

Upside gap two crows is a bearish three-day reversal pattern that occurs only in uptrends. It is identified by the strong upward movement on the first day followed by a gap higher on the second day, with an even weaker close following a positive start to the third day. This shows that the uptrend has definitely stalled due to increased selling activity. The key here is that the gap between the first and second days remains open even after the third day. The second and third days are black candles, which is where the reference to crows comes from. This pattern starts out like an evening star with the gap higher between the first and second days.

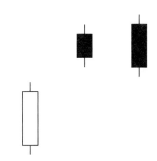

FIGURE 4-37 • Upside Gap Two Crows

This is not an overly bearish pattern as shown when the candles are combined (Fig. 4-38), which means some form of confirmation is vital before entering a trade on this pattern.

The daily chart of The Boeing Co (Fig. 4-39) shows an example of the upside gap two crows pattern. There are five pieces to the development of this pattern.

1. Price is in an uptrend.

2. The second day opens with a gap higher followed by a close below the open but the gap is unfilled.

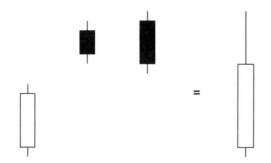

**Upside gap two crows forms a long
upper shadow when combined.**

FIGURE 4-38 • Upside Gap Two Crows Combined

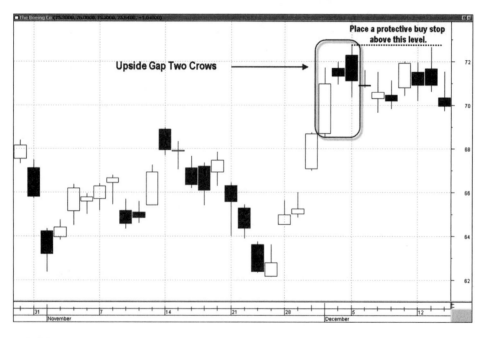

FIGURE 4-39 • Upside Gap Two Crows: The Boeing Co., Daily

Source: MetaStock

3. Price gaps higher on the third day but closes below the close of the second day.

4. The third day's candle engulfs the second day, but the gap still remains open.

5. This shows that even though the gap remains open, upside progress has been stalled.

When trading this pattern, it is best to wait for a close below the open gap, which fills the gap and signals that a reversal lower is under way. Place a protective buy stop above the highest point of the formation, usually the high of the third candle in the pattern.

Three Inside Up and Three Inside Down

The *three inside up* and *three inside down* patterns (Fig. 4-40) are not found in any Japanese literature and were developed by Greg Morris to be used as confirmation of harami reversals. In each case, the first two days form a harami pattern with the third day providing reversal confirmation on a closing basis. For example, a bullish harami pattern followed by a close higher on the third day would constitute a three inside up pattern while a bearish harami pattern followed by a lower close would constitute a three inside down pattern.

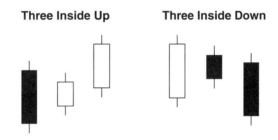

Three Inside Up **Three Inside Down**

FIGURE 4-40 • Three Inside Up and Three Inside Down

The close in the forecast direction of the harami not only confirms the reversal but also forms a bullish hammer on the three inside up or a bearish shooting star on the three inside down as shown in Fig. 4-41.

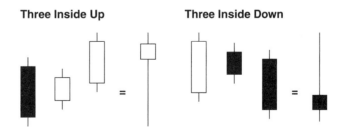

Three Inside Up **Three Inside Down**

Here three inside up and three inside down are combined.

FIGURE 4-41 • Three Inside Up and Three Inside Down Combined

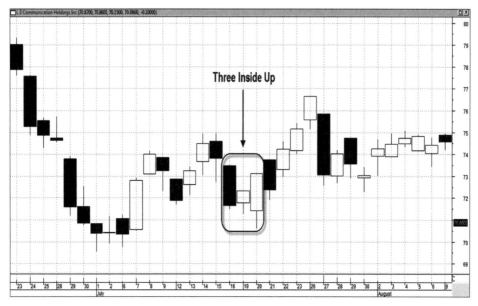

FIGURE 4-42 • Three Inside Up: L3 Communications Holdings Inc., Daily
Source: MetaStock

The three inside up pattern is shown in the daily chart of L3 Communications Holdings Inc. (Fig. 4-42). Notice that the first two days of the pattern are a classic bullish harami, and the third day closes above the close of the second candle. The pattern develops in four steps.

1. Price is in a downtrend.
2. A long black candle forms, confirming the downtrend.
3. A bullish white harami candle forms, which demonstrates that downside momentum is weakening.
4. Price reverses higher, forming a white candle that closes higher than the harami candle, confirming the reversal.

The higher the close the more bullish is the reversal. If the close can make it above the high of the first (black) candle, that is a more powerful reversal signal.

The three inside down confirms a bearish harami reversal as shown in the daily chart of Public Entertainment Group Inc. (Fig. 4-43). This pattern can be broken down into four parts.

1. Price is in an uptrend.
2. A long white candle forms, confirming the uptrend.
3. A bearish black harami candle forms, showing that upside momentum is waning.
4. Price reverses lower, forming a black candle that closes lower than the harami candle, which confirms the reversal.

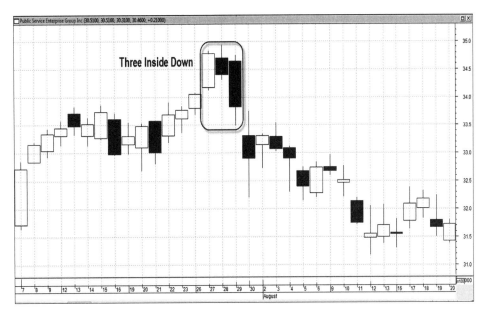

FIGURE 4-43 • Three Inside Down: Public Service Entertainment Group Inc., Daily
Source: MetaStock

Three Outside Up and Three Outside Down

The *three outside up* and *three outside down* patterns (Fig. 4-44) were also developed by Greg Morris, this time to confirm reversals relating to engulfing patterns. The concept is the same as three inside up and three inside down in that a close in the direction of the forecast reversal is needed for confirmation.

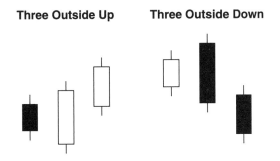

FIGURE 4-44 • Three Outside Up and Three Outside Down

When combined, these patterns form a line similar to a hammer in the three outside up, or a line similar to a shooting star in the three outside down. The word *similar* is used because these patterns result in slightly longer real bodies than for the classic hammer or shooting star lines.

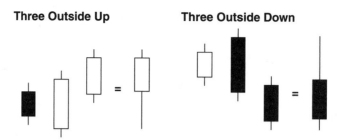

Three Outside Up   **Three Outside Down**

**When combined, these patterns form lines
similar to a hammer and a shooting star.**

FIGURE 4-45 • Three Outside Up and Three Outside Down Combined

The daily chart of Newmont Mining Corp. (Fig. 4-46) shows an example of a three outside up pattern

1. Price is in a downtrend.
2. A black candle forms, although it has a rather long lower shadow, which hints that a reversal may be near.
3. A white engulfing candle forms.
4. On the third day a white candle forms that closes above the engulfing candle, confirming the reversal.

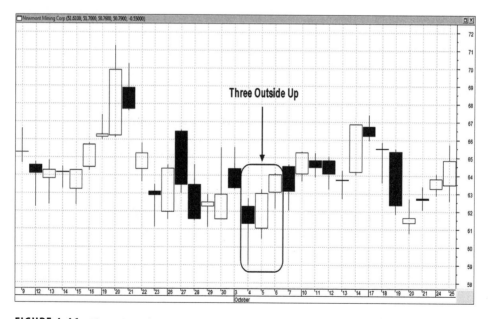

FIGURE 4-46 • Three Outside Up: Newmont Mining Corp., Daily
Source: MetaStock

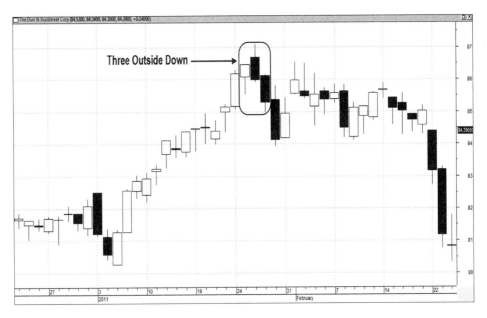

FIGURE 4-47 • Three Outside Down: The Dun & Bradstreet Corp., Daily
Source: MetaStock

The three outside down pattern confirms a bearish reversal off of a high. The daily chart of The Dunn & Bradstreet Corp. (Fig. 4-47) shows an example of a three outside down pattern. The pattern develops in four stages.

1. Price is in an up trend.
2. A white candle forms, confirming the uptrend.
3. A black engulfing candle forms, which signals that a reversal lower is likely.
4. On the third day a second black candle forms that closes below the engulfing candle, confirming the reversal.

A number of reversal patterns were covered in this chapter. You should be familiar with these patterns as they have the possibility of being "trend enders," or patterns that have strong reversal implications when encountered. These patterns, along with the continuation patterns that will be covered in Chapter 5 and Sakata's strategies (Chapter 6), form the foundation for effective candlestick pattern analysis. We will then move on and combine these building blocks with more modern methods of price analysis using momentum indicators and volume to develop a weight of the evidence trading methodology. By developing a stout working knowledge of each piece, you will see that combining patterns and methodologies achieves a powerful synergy.

Summary

- The appearance of a reversal pattern is no guarantee that the trend will reverse.
- It is always wise to wait for price to confirm a reversal before entering a trade based on these patterns.
- No reversal pattern is valid unless there is a trend in place to reverse.
- Stop placement should always be a consideration when placing a trade based on these patterns.
- It is important to understand the psychology behind each pattern as it unfolds.

QUIZ

1. **A valid candlestick reversal pattern guarantees a change in price direction.**
   A. True
   B. False

2. **Candlestick reversal patterns are valid and reliable in**
   A. Trending markets
   B. Volatile or choppy markets
   C. Sideways or consolidating markets
   D. All of the above

3. **When trading candlestick reversal patterns**
   A. It is safe to assume that the pattern will be successful
   B. Trade the pattern before completion to get a jump on other traders
   C. Always wait for price to confirm the reversal
   D. Stops are not necessary and should rarely be used

4. **When learning candlestick reversal patterns, it is best to**
   A. Understand the psychology behind the pattern
   B. Understand trend direction when identifying the patterns
   C. Understand that they reflect a short-term change in trader psychology
   D. All of the above

5. **What candlestick reversal pattern is shown in the chart below?**

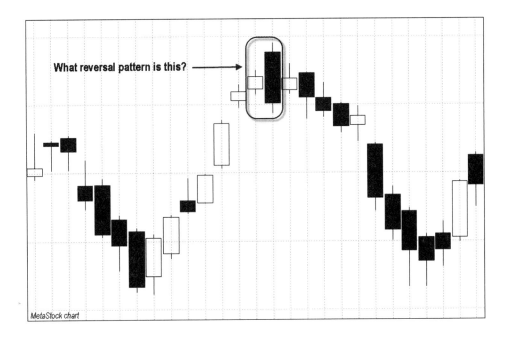

What reversal pattern is this?

MetaStock chart

A. Bearish harami
B. Dark cloud cover
C. Evening star
D. Bearish engulfing pattern

6. **What candlestick reversal pattern is shown in the chart below?**

What reversal pattern is this? ⟶

MetaStock chart

A. Bearish harami
B. Upside gap two crows
C. Evening star
D. Morning star

7. **Which reversal pattern appears in an uptrend?**
    A. Piercing line
    B. Bullish engulfing
    C. Dark cloud cover
    D. Morning star

8. **Which reversal pattern appears in a downtrend?**
    A. Evening star
    B. Dark cloud cover
    C. Morning star
    D. Hanging man

9. What candlestick reversal pattern is in the chart below?

What reversal pattern is this? ⟶

MetaStock chart

    A. Evening star
    B. Shooting star
    C. Bullish harami
    D. Upside gap two crows

10. A piercing line is a valid reversal pattern in a downtrend.
    A. True
    B. False

Chapter **5**

Candlestick Continuation Patterns

Candlestick continuation patterns represent a period of rest, or consolidation, in an existing trend. The formation of these patterns indicates that the side driving the trend (buyers in an uptrend or sellers in a downtrend) is taking a breather by either locking in profits or waiting for slightly better levels at which to buy or sell.

CHAPTER OBJECTIVES

In this chapter, you will

- Learn the purpose of continuation patterns
- Identify the types of continuation patterns
- Confirm continuation patterns
- Understand trading examples of continuation patterns

The advantage of identifying and trading with continuation patterns is that they can give a trader a safer entry point at which to either jump on the trend if an earlier opportunity was missed or to add to existing positions. Entering positions in this fashion gives a trader a chance to harness market energy that already exists and is moving in the direction of the trend.

Just like the reversal patterns discussed in Chapter 4, it is always best for price to confirm the resumption of the trend before jumping into a trade. Assuming that a continuation pattern will resolve itself in the direction of the trend can lead to premature trade entry, which causes unnecessary trading losses. Another point to remember is that it is always wise to be mindful of the trend. Any of these patterns that appear in a choppy or trendless market have little meaning. This chapter will discuss continuation patterns, while trends will be covered in Chapter 7. Just as with the reversal patterns covered in Chapter 4, each continuation pattern discussed in this chapter will be identified, the trader mindset will be explained, and a real chart example will be shown.

Windows

In candlestick charting, a *window* is the same as a gap in Western technical analysis. It is an open spot or a break on a price chart that forms between the close of one day and the opening of the next. Windows are typically emotional events that are driven by news stories, earnings reports, changes in management, etc., that cause trader sentiment to intensify in either a positive or negative direction.

In candlestick terminology, the opening of a gap is referred to as "opening the window," while the filling of a gap is referred to as "closing the window." A gap formed to the upside is known as a "rising window," while a gap that forms to the downside is known as a "falling window." Think of a rising window as a sudden positive shift in trader sentiment, while a falling window represents a sudden negative shift in trader sentiment.

The reason that windows are included in a chapter on continuation patterns is that their formation creates areas of support (rising window) or resistance (falling window) on a price chart that should allow price movement to continue in the direction of the open window. A breach of an open window in the opposite direction indicates a trend reversal may be under way. One advantage of windows is that their formation allows for a clear, unambiguous area for stop loss order placement. If the stop loss level is reached, then the support or resistance level delineated by the open window is no longer valid, which shows a change in market characteristics and likely changes the reason for holding a position in the first place.

In order for an open window to be identified, the entire candle is used. In other words, there must be no overlap of any kind between the candles, including the shadows. Figure 5-1 shows the characteristics of rising and falling windows.

The daily chart of NVIDIA Corp. (Fig. 5-2) shows four examples of windows on one chart. The first instance on the left side of the chart is an example of a falling window, which showed an increase in bearish behavior on the part of traders. The window remained open for three days before being closed by a long white candle, which signified that a price reversal higher was taking hold. Also

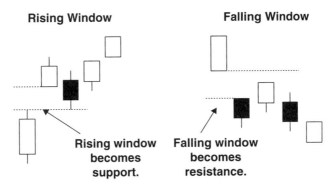

Rising Window   **Falling Window**

Rising window becomes support.   Falling window becomes resistance.

FIGURE 5-1 • Rising and Falling Windows

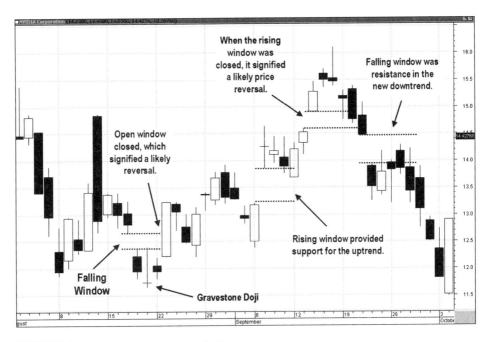

FIGURE 5-2 • Windows: NVIDIA Corp., Daily
Source: MetaStock

notice the gravestone doji that formed two days after the formation of the falling window. The long white candle that closed the window merely confirmed the reversal that had been suggested by the appearance of the doji. The closure of the open falling window provided extra confirmation.

Next take a look at the second window identified. That is an example of a rising window that shows a sharp increase in bullish sentiment among traders. That window provided support, which meant that the upward push was likely to continue. The third example is another rising window, only this time the window was filled five days later as price reversed lower. The fourth example shows a falling window that remained open, providing resistance as price moved lower.

In order for a window to be closed, the candle prior to the opening of the window must be "touched" by a subsequent candle at some point. If any part of the window remains open, the support or resistance characteristics of the window are still in effect. It is also possible for a window to be closed, but then the existing trend resumes. That is known as "taking care of business" as price goes back to fill the gap before resuming the trend. It is when price moves *past* the origin of the window that a price reversal is likely.

When using open windows as entry points in the trend, a protective stop order should be placed just below the lower extreme of a rising window in an uptrend or just above the upper extreme of a falling window in a downtrend.

Tasuki Gaps

A *tasuki gap* (Fig. 5-3) is a three-day candle pattern that includes an open window. This pattern gets its name because it contains what is known in Japanese literature as a *tasuki line*. A tasuki line is formed following a white candle when the next day opens within the real body of the white candle and closes below its low. The same is true on the downside, when a black candle is followed by a candle that opens within its real body and closes above its high. This is an important concept to understand as it forms the basis for days two and three of this pattern.

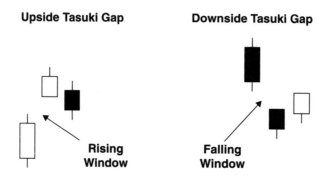

FIGURE 5-3 • Tasuki Gaps

When the candles that form a tasuki gap are combined (Fig. 5-4), the result is a long white candle in the upside tasuki gap (bullish) and a long black candle in a downside tasuki gap (bearish). While the long candles typically reinforce the trend, the long shadows in the opposite direction take away some of the strength of this combined pattern. The psychology behind the pattern is rather elementary—simply trade in the direction of the open window.

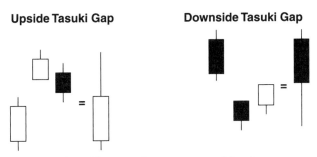

Upside Tasuki Gap   **Downside Tasuki Gap**

Tasuki gap patterns are combined.

FIGURE 5-4 • Tasuki Gaps Combined

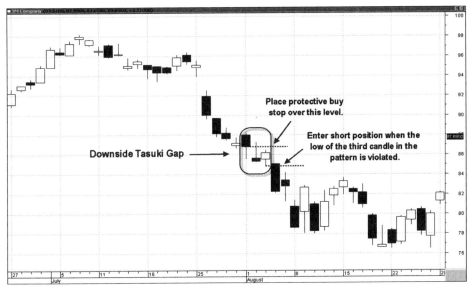

FIGURE 5-5 • Downside Tasuki Gap: 3M Corp., Daily

Source: MetaStock

The daily chart of 3M Corp. (Fig. 5-5) shows an example of a downside tasuki gap. The pattern developed in six stages.

1. The stock is in a downtrend as demonstrated by the falling price.
2. On the first day of the pattern, price forms a black candle, reinforcing the trend.
3. The second day gaps away from the first candle, opening a falling window.
4. On the third day, price opens within the real body of the second candle and then closes above the high
5. In spite of the efforts of buyers, there is not enough strength to close the window.
6. The downtrend resumes on the fourth day as a long black candle is formed.

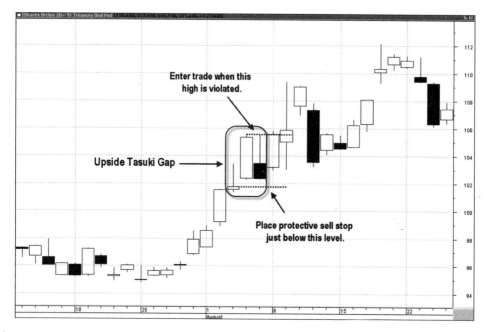

FIGURE 5-6 · Upside Tasuki Gap: iShares Barclays 20+ Treasury Bond ETF., Daily
Source: MetaStock

The fact that the window could not be closed is a show of weakness, which emboldens the sellers and the downtrend resumes.

When trading a downside tasuki gap, a protective buy stop should be placed above the high point of the open window. The trade should be entered when the lowest point of the second or third day is violated.

The daily chart of the iShares Barclays 20+ Treasury Bond ETF (Fig. 5-6) shows an example of an upside tasuki gap.

1. Price is in an uptrend.
2. On the first day of the pattern, a candle forms that looks like an inverted hammer.
3. Price gaps higher on the second day, negating the potential reversal the inverted hammer showed.
4. On the third day price opens within the body of the candle and then closes at the low.
5. In spite of the efforts of sellers, there is not enough strength to close the window.
6. The uptrend resumes on the fourth day when a long white candle is formed.

Since there was not enough selling pressure to close the open window, buyers were emboldened and the uptrend resumed.

Notice in the previous example that the first day of the tasuki gap pattern was actually an inverted hammer. The point to remember here is that even though the inverted hammer looked ominous at the time, *no reversal was confirmed*, which meant that the uptrend was still in place and had to be respected. The rising window formed at the open the next day confirmed the will of the traders and the strength of the trend. When trading an upside tasuki gap, a protective sell stop should be placed below the low point of the open window. The trade should be entered when the highest point between the second and third days is violated.

It is important to note that there is another continuation pattern that closely resembles the tasuki gap, called the rising and falling three methods. The difference between the patterns is that in the three method patterns, the gap is closed on the third day, which would normally signal a reversal of trend rather than a continuation. Rather than present this seemingly conflicting pattern here, it will be presented in Chapter 6 when Sakata's strategies are covered. The explanation there should help you properly interpret the pattern.

Separating Lines

Separating lines (Fig. 5-7) are strong continuation patterns that use the same concept as meeting lines (covered in Chapter 4), but only in the opposite direction. Recall that meeting lines form a reversal pattern in which two consecutive opposite colored candles have the same closing price. Separating lines are formed when prices have the same *opening* price but move in the opposite direction. For example, in an uptrend this would appear as a black candle followed by a white candle that opens at the same price as the black candle opening but continues higher in the direction of the prevailing trend. Make sure that you do not bypass this pattern simply because the opening prices are not an exact match. As long as the opening prices are within a few ticks of each other that would be deemed close enough.

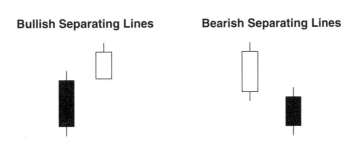

Bullish Separating Lines   **Bearish Separating Lines**

**It is important for the opening prices to be the same
or very close. Do not bypass this pattern just
because the opening prices are not an exact match.**

FIGURE 5-7 • Separating Lines

When combined, the candles that form the separating lines each show a bias in the direction of the trend (Fig. 5-8). Notice that the bullish separating lines form a white candle with a long lower shadow while the bearish separating lines reduce to a black candle with a long upper shadow.

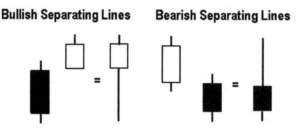

FIGURE 5-8 • Separating Lines Combined

The daily chart of Bank of America Corp. (Fig. 5-9) shows an example of bullish separating lines. There are four parts to the psychology of this pattern.

1. Price is in an uptrend.
2. The first day of the pattern is a black candle, which gives buyers pause.
3. The second day sees a gap higher open as price opens at the same level as the previous day.
4. A white candle is formed, signaling that the uptrend is likely to continue.

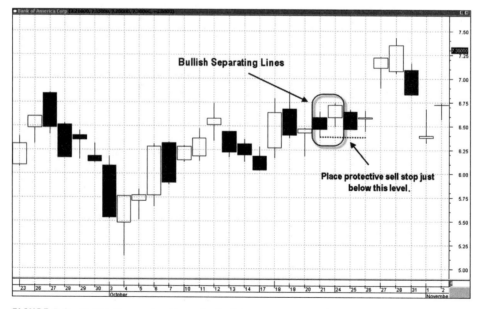

FIGURE 5-9 • Bullish Separating Lines: Bank of America Corp., Daily
Source: MetaStock

Even though it is not an open window on the chart, the opening price on the second day does create a gap higher because the opening price is considerably higher than the previous day's closing price. This also backs up the adage used when trading the tasuki gap, which says to trade in the direction of the gap.

When trading this pattern, a protective stop should be placed below the low of the first (black) candle of the pattern. It is permissible to enter the trade near the close of the second day once it is apparent that separating lines have formed, or for a more conservative approach, one can wait until the high of the second (white) candle is violated.

The daily chart of Pan American Silver Corp. (Fig. 5-10) shows an example of bearish separating lines. The pattern develops in four parts.

1. Price is in a downtrend.
2. The first day of the pattern is a white candle, which gives short sellers pause.
3. The second day sees price gap lower to open at the same price as the previous day.
4. A black candle is formed, signaling the downtrend is likely to continue.

When trading this pattern, a protective buy stop should be placed over the high of the first (white) candle of the pattern. When entering a short trade, it is permissible to enter as near to the close of the second day as possible once it is certain that the pattern will form. For a more conservative approach, wait until the low of the second (black) candle has been violated.

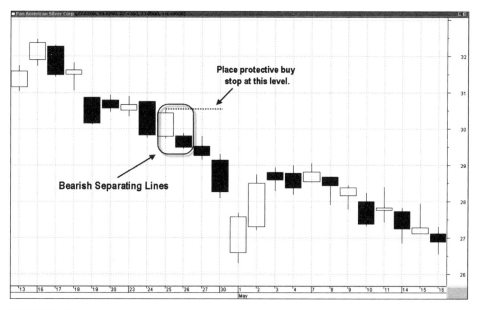

FIGURE 5-10 • Bearish Separating Lines: Pan American Silver Corp., Daily
Source: MetaStock

Neck Lines

Neck lines are continuation patterns that begin forming what look to be either a piercing line or dark cloud cover reversal. The difference with these patterns is that they do not penetrate into the real body of the previous candle. Their inability to do so means that countertrend pressure was not strong enough to get into the previous real body at all, which bodes well for the continuation of the trend. The two neck lines we will examine are the in-neck and on-neck lines.

When I first began using candlesticks, I had trouble distinguishing these two neck line patterns from one another. Perhaps the best way to think about these is to visualize any shadow on the candle as a "neck." If the real body closes inside the shadow and at or very near the closing price of the previous candle, it is inside the neck or "in neck." Conversely, if the second candle closes at the extreme of the shadow of the first candle, then it is on the neck, or "on neck."

An *in-neck line* (Fig. 5-11) is a continuation pattern that gaps in the direction of the trend only to see countertrend forces push the price in the opposite direction for a close against the trend. The close is at or near the closing price of the previous day's candle. The lack of a strong push to get the price into the real body of the preceding candle is a signal that countertrend forces are not strong enough to cause a full price reversal. This reinforces the strength of the prevailing trend, which is expected to resume.

Bullish In-Neck Line   **Bearish In-Neck Line**

The in-neck line closes at or very near the previous candle's close.

FIGURE 5-11 • In-Neck Lines

When combined (Fig. 5-12), the candles that make up a neck line reinforce the trend direction. For example, the bullish in-neck line is comprised of a long white candle with a longer upper shadow, and the bearish in-neck line is comprised of a long black candle with a longer lower shadow.

Bullish In-Neck Line   **Bearish In-Neck Line**

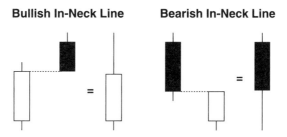

FIGURE 5-12 • In-Neck Lines Combined

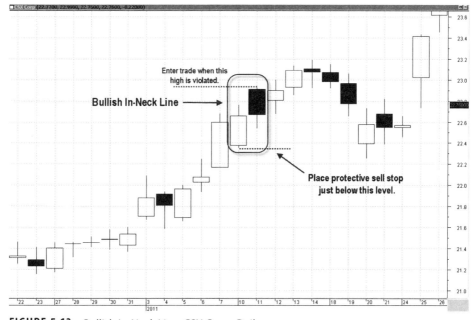

FIGURE 5-13 • Bullish In-Neck Line: CSX Corp., Daily
Source: MetaStock

The daily chart of CSX Corp. (Fig. 5-13) shows an example of a bullish in-neck line. The psychology behind this pattern can be described in six steps.

1. Price is in an uptrend.
2. The first day forms a white candle, which confirms the uptrend.
3. The second day gaps higher but reverses lower to close near the previous day's close.
4. The lack of penetration into the first day's real body shows the weakness of the reversal.
5. This emboldens the bulls, who gap the opening price higher the following day.
6. Price continues to move higher.

FIGURE 5-14 • Bearish In-Neck Line: FedEx Corp., Daily
Source: MetaStock

When trading the bullish in-neck line, a protective sell stop should be placed just below the low of the first day of the pattern. A new trading position can be initiated when the high of the second day is violated.

A bearish in-neck line appears in a downtrend. The daily chart of FedEx Corp. (Fig. 5-14) shows an example of the pattern. It can be broken down in six parts.

1. Price is in a downtrend.
2. The first day forms a black candle, which reinforces the downtrend.
3. The second day gaps lower but reverses higher to close near the first day's close.
4. This lack of penetration into the first day's real body shows the weakness of the reversal.
5. This emboldens the bears, who gap the opening price lower the following day.
6. Price continues to move lower.

When trading the bearish in-neck line, a protective buy stop should be placed just above the high of the first day of the pattern. A new trading position can be initiated when the low of the second day is violated.

On-neck lines (Fig. 5-15) are patterns that have second day reversals only up to the extreme of the prior day's shadow. In other words, the reversal was so weak that it could not penetrate into the previous day's range at all.

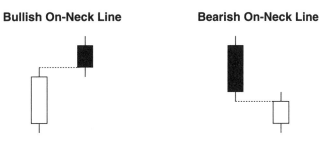

**On-neck lines close at or near the high
or low of the previous candle.**

FIGURE 5-15 • On-Neck Lines

When combined these lines give a more bullish or bearish look (Fig. 5-16), depending on the direction of the trend. In the bullish on-neck line, the product is a longer white candle than the in-neck line, while the bearish on-neck line produces a more bearish looking black candle than its in-neck counterpart.

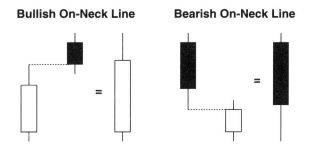

**When combined, these patterns have a slightly more
bullish or bearish look than the in-neck lines.**

FIGURE 5-16 • On-Neck Lines Combined

The daily chart of Expedia Inc. (Fig. 5-17) shows an example of a bullish on-neck line.

1. Price is in an uptrend.
2. The first day forms a white candle, which reinforces the uptrend.
3. The second day gaps higher but reverses lower, closing at the high point of the first day.
4. This lack of penetration into the first day's range shows the weakness of the reversal.

FIGURE 5-17 • Bullish On-Neck Line: Expedia Inc., Daily
Source: MetaStock

   5. This emboldens the bulls, who gap the opening price higher the following day.

   6. After a brief pullback, price continues to move higher.

Again, when trading this pattern, a protective sell stop should be placed below the low of the first day of the pattern. Price confirmation is necessary before entering a new position.

A bearish on-neck line occurs in a downtrend and is a signal that the downtrend is strong and will continue. The daily chart of Home Depot Inc. (Fig. 5-18) shows an example of a bearish on-neck line. The formation of the pattern can be described in six stages.

   1. Price is in a downtrend.

   2. The first day forms a black candle, which reinforces the downtrend.

   3. The second day gaps lower but reverses higher, closing at the low point of the first day.

   4. This lack of penetration into the first day's range shows the weakness of the reversal.

   5. This emboldens the bears, who gap the opening price lower the following day.

   6. Price continues to move lower.

FIGURE 5-18 • Bearish On-Neck Line: Home Depot Inc., Daily
Source: MetaStock

When trading this pattern, a protective buy stop should be placed above the high of the first day of the pattern. A new trading position can be initiated when the low of the second day is violated.

Thrusting Lines

A *thrusting line* (Fig. 5-19) is one step beyond the in-neck line as the closing price is into the real body of the prior day's candle but not to the halfway point of the real body to trigger a reversal signal. This two-day pattern begins the same way as neck lines, with the first day moving in the direction of the trend while the

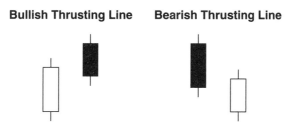

Bullish Thrusting Line   Bearish Thrusting Line

The reversal of the second candle does not reach the halfway point of the first candle's real body, showing a lack of resolve among traders.

FIGURE 5-19 • Thrusting Lines

second day gaps open in the same direction before reversing and closing within the real body of the first day. Since the close is not at least halfway into the real body of the first candle, a valid dark cloud cover or piercing line is not formed.

When the two lines are combined (Fig. 5-20), thrusting lines do not produce overwhelmingly bullish or bearish looking candles. The bullish thrusting line forms a white candle with a long upper shadow while the bearish thrusting line forms a black candle with a long lower shadow.

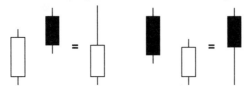

FIGURE 5-20 • Thrusting Lines Combined

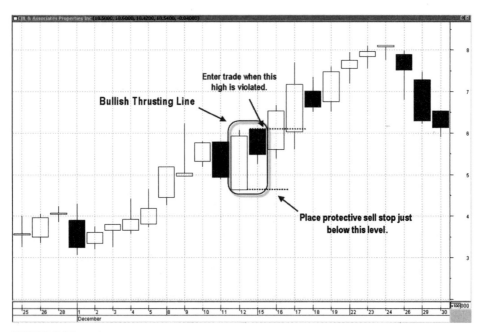

FIGURE 5-21 • Bullish Thrusting Line: CBL & Associates Properties Inc., Daily
Source: MetaStock

A bullish thrusting line occurs in uptrends and signifies that a potential reversal lower lacked the selling pressure to stop the price advance. The daily chart of CBL & Associates Properties Inc. (Fig. 5-21) shows an example of a bullish thrusting line. This pattern has six parts.

1. Price is in an uptrend.
2. The first day forms a white candle, which reinforces the uptrend.

3. The second day gaps higher and opens above the previous day's high but reverses lower.

4. The reversal penetrates the real body of the previous day but does not make it to the halfway point to give a valid reversal signal.

5. The weak selling pressure emboldens the bulls.

6. A long white candle is formed the next day as the uptrend continues.

When trading the bullish thrusting pattern, a protective sell stop should be placed below the low of the first day of the pattern. A new trading position can be initiated when the high of the second day (black candle) is violated, which shows that the uptrend is resuming.

A bearish thrusting line occurs in a downtrend and demonstrates a lack of buying pressure needed to reverse the decline. The daily chart of Market Vectors Steel ETF (Fig. 5-22) shows an example of a bearish thrusting line.

1. Price is in a downtrend.

2. The first day forms a black candle, which reinforces the downtrend.

3. The second day gaps lower and opens below the previous day's low but reverses higher.

4. The reversal penetrates the real body of the previous day but does not make it to the halfway point.

5. The weak buying pressure emboldens the bears.

6. A long black candle is formed the next day as the downtrend continues.

FIGURE 5-22 • Bearish Thrusting Line: Market Vectors Steel ETF, Daily
Source: MetaStock

When trading the bearish thrusting pattern, a protective buy stop should be placed above the high of the first day of the pattern. A new trading position can be initiated when the low of the second day (white candle) is violated, which shows that the downtrend is resuming.

The main thing to remember about neck lines and thrusting lines is that while in each case price gaps open in the direction of the trend on the second day and then reverse against the trend, it is the degree of the reversal that must be watched. In other words, countertrend forces gained control of the price action after the open but were unable to exert enough force to trigger a reversal signal. Japanese candlesticks are different from conventional bar charts in that much emphasis is placed on the real body—or the difference between the opening and closing prices. So while a gap in the direction of the trend followed by an intra-day reversal may seem like a countertrend move, the fact that the countertrend forces were not able to apply enough force to penetrate at least halfway into the previous day's real body bodes well for the continuation of the existing price trend.

Still Struggling?

Neck and thrusting lines are continuation patterns and not reversal patterns.

One of the hardest things for me to get straight when I began using candle-sticks was that neck lines and thrusting lines were continuation—not reversal patterns. It seems intuitive that if a price gap opens in the direction of the trend and then reverses *against* the trend, countertrend forces are making a stand. The key to remember is how far the reversal penetrates the real body of the preceding candle—if it penetrates it at all. In order to be classified as a reversal pattern, the reversal candle must penetrate at least halfway into the real body of the preceding candle, which would produce a dark cloud cover reversal, or an engulfing pattern if the reversal "engulfs" the entire previous real body. When countertrend forces cannot muster enough strength to pen-etrate the halfway point of the previous candle, those trading in the direction of the trend are emboldened, which should lead to a resumption of the trend.

Rising and Falling Three Methods

The *rising and falling three methods* (Fig. 5-23) contain periods of sharp price movement followed by a period of consolidation, or "rest." The rest period repre-sented in these patterns is similar to the ones found in such Western technical analysis patterns as the flag or the Gann pullback. The three days after a sharp price move represent a quiet period where some traders lock in profits, but this action does not cause enough countertrend force to trigger a full trend reversal.

Rising Three Method   **Falling Three Method**

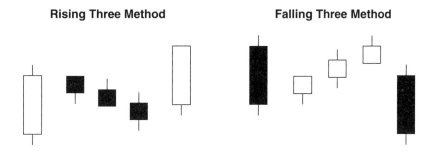

This method can consist of at least two or more than three "consolidation" candles and still be valid.

FIGURE 5-23 • Rising and Falling Three Methods

When the candles that make up the pattern are combined (Fig. 5-24), the rising three method reduces to a long white candle, while the falling three method reduces to a long black candle. These reinforce the strength of the prevailing trend.

Rising Three Method   **Falling Three Method**

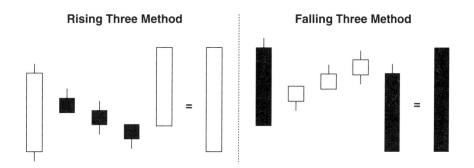

FIGURE 5-24 • Rising and Falling Three Methods Combined

The rising three method begins with a long white candle in an uptrend that is followed by a three-day consolidation within the high-low range of the white candle, which includes the shadows. A "perfect" consolidation pattern should consist of three small bodied black candles that form a downward pattern. Of course we have already seen that not every pattern develops in a perfect text-book fashion. This means that the consolidation days should primarily be small bodied and their own real bodies must be within the total range of the first day. Whether they are descending black candles is of less importance. The consolidation pattern can also consist of at least two and possibly more than three days of consolidation. Again, the thing to look for is that the candles must remain within the range of the first long white candle. The final candle of the pattern opens above the close of the previous reaction day and closes at a new high for the pattern.

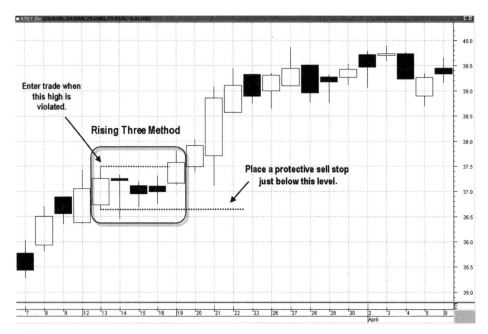

FIGURE 5-25 • Rising Three Method: AT&T Inc., Daily

Source: MetaStock

The daily chart of AT&T Inc. (Fig. 5-25) shows an example of a rising three method. The pattern can be broken down into five stages.

1. Price is in an uptrend.
2. A long white candle forms, which reinforces the strength of the uptrend.
3. Price consolidates within the full range of the white candle for the next three days.
4. On the next day, price gaps higher at the open and makes a new high for the pattern.
5. The uptrend resumes.

When trading this pattern, a position can be taken when price breaks through the high of the white candle that started the pattern. A protective sell stop should be placed below the low of that same white candle.

The falling three method begins with a long black candle in a downtrend that is followed by a three-day price consolidation contained by the high-low range of the first day's black candle. Price then gaps lower at the open of the fourth day, and price sets a new low for the pattern, signifying that the downtrend has resumed. Just as with the rising three method, the three-day consolidation can be as few as two days or more than three days as long as they are all contained within the high-low range of the first day.

FIGURE 5-26 • Falling Three Method: Google Inc., Daily
Source: MetaStock

The daily chart of Google Inc. (Fig. 5-26) is an example of a falling three method.

1. Price is in a downtrend.
2. A long black candle forms, which reinforces the strength of the downtrend.
3. Price consolidates within the full range of the black candle for the next three days.
4. On the next day, price moves lower and makes a new low for the pattern.
5. The downtrend resumes.

When trading this pattern, a position can be taken when price breaks through the low of the black candle that started the pattern. A protective buy stop should be placed above the high of the initial black candle.

Summary

- Continuation patterns represent periods of rest, or consolidation, in the market.
- Continuation patterns provide good opportunities for traders to enter the trend.

- It is always wise to wait for confirmation that the trend has resumed before entering a trade.
- Stop loss orders should be used on every trade.
- A tasuki gap is a continuation pattern based on an open gap or window in the direction of the trend.
- Separating lines are opposite colored lines that have the same opening price.
- Neck lines and the thrusting line are failed piercing line or dark cloud cover patterns.
- The thrusting line penetrates the real body of the previous candle while neck lines do not.
- The on-neck line closes at the extreme high or low of the previous candle depending on trend direction.
- The in-neck line closes at or near the closing price of the previous candle.
- The rising and falling three methods are formed by a sharp price movement followed by a period (three days) of rest.

QUIZ

1. **Continuation patterns represent**
   A. Periods of high emotion
   B. Periods of rest, or consolidation, in an existing trend
   C. Periods when trading should be avoided
   D. Periods when trading opportunities have been missed

2. **Windows are also known as what in Western trading?**
   A. Open trades
   B. Periods where market analysis is seen very clearly
   C. Gaps
   D. None of the above

3. **A tasuki line consists of**
   A. A line following a white candle that opens in the real body of the white candle and closes below its low
   B. An open window followed by a black candle
   C. A "line in the sand" that differentiates between trends
   D. All of the above

4. **Which statement is true regarding windows?**
   A. A rising window provides support while a falling window provides resistance.
   B. Windows show periods of high emotion.
   C. Their formation provides a clear level for stop placement.
   D. All of the above

5. **Which continuation pattern consists of consecutive candles that have the same opening price but move in the opposite direction?**
   A. Meeting lines
   B. In-neck lines
   C. Separating lines
   D. On-neck lines

6. **Which pattern is a failed piercing line or dark cloud cover pattern?**
   A. In-neck line
   B. On-neck line
   C. Thrusting pattern
   D. All of the above

7. **Which of these patterns penetrates the real body of the previous candle?**
   A. In-neck line
   B. On-neck line
   C. Thrusting pattern
   D. All of the above

8. **Which continuation pattern consists of a sharp price move followed by three days of rest?**
   A. Tasuki gap
   B. Separating lines
   C. Thrusting line
   D. Rising or falling three methods

9. **When trading continuation patterns, it is wise to**
   A. Ignore the trend
   B. Jump into a trade as soon as the pattern appears
   C. Not use stops since the trend is established
   D. Wait for confirmation of trend resumption before entering a trade

10. **What is the main psychology behind the tasuki gap pattern?**
   A. Wait for the window to be closed before entering the trade.
   B. Trade in the direction of the open gap.
   C. The opening of the gap is reason enough to go long—nothing else is needed to enter a trade.
   D. None of the above

Chapter **6**

Sakata's Strategies and Longer Term Candle Patterns

Sakata's strategies form the basis for modern-day candle pattern analysis. Understanding these patterns and the psychology behind them can give a trader a better understanding of the psychology, or mood, of the market, which can lead to better trading decisions

CHAPTER OBJECTIVES

In this chapter, you will

- Learn Sakata's strategies and the psychology that each represents
- Discover how Sakata's strategies form the basis for previously covered patterns
- Understand longer term candle patterns that can signal longer term reversals
- Combine longer term patterns with shorter term reversal patterns

The number three has been considered a mysterious number with mystical powers dating back to ancient Japan. It is no wonder that Sakata's strategies rely heavily on this number. These strategies were developed by Munehisa Honma. (Some references to this legendary trader list his first name as Sohkyu and others as Munehisa.)

Honma and some of the methods he used were introduced in Chapter 1. This chapter delves a little deeper into the strategies and presents some of the price patterns he used in his analysis to amass his great fortune. These patterns are taken from the 160 rules that Honma penned at age 51. While Honma did not personally use candlestick charts, the pattern recognition methods contained in these strategies are instrumental in the analysis methods used in candlestick charting today.

The reason these strategies are named "Sakata's strategies" and not "Honma's strategies" is because Honma hailed from Sakata. Other names used to describe these strategies are the Honma constitution, Sakata's five methods, and Sakata's laws.

Sakata's Strategies

As mentioned, Sakata's five strategies involve the mystical number three. The word *San* in each description means "three." There are five strategies.

- San-zan—Three Mountains
- San-sen—Three Rivers
- San-ku—Three Gaps
- San-pei—Three Soldiers
- San-poh—Three Methods

In previous chapters, we have concentrated on the size, colors, and patterns of the candles that show potential price reversals. Now we will step back and look at the broader picture, as these reversal patterns have longer term implications for trend direction. After examining Sakata's five strategies in detail, we will look at some other larger scale reversal patterns.

Three Mountains

The *three mountains* pattern invokes the concept of resistance, which is discussed in more detail in Chapter 7. Basically, resistance is an area where sellers emerge because they no longer see adequate value for the stock or commodity being traded at a certain price level, which repels any further price advances. These areas can be easily spotted on a price chart. In this case, three mountains is a pattern where price attempted and failed to break through a zone or area of price resistance on three different occasions, causing price to change direction and move lower. Each of the three peaks can be in the same vicinity, or they can form a series of lower tops as each successive peak weakens.

A variation of three mountains is the *three Buddha top*. This pattern is similar to the Western *head and shoulders* reversal pattern. The three Buddha top differs from three mountains in that this pattern requires a certain pattern—in other words it does not have as loose a definition as the three mountains pattern. The three Buddha top requires that the second of the three peaks be the highest, with the first and third peaks making lower highs. In addition, the first and third peaks should be near the same price level with regard to each other. This pattern gets its name from a Buddhist temple where one large Buddha is placed between two smaller Buddhas. Figure 6-1 shows examples of the three mountains and three Buddha top.

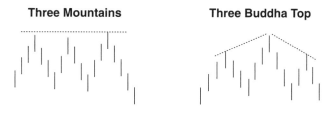

Three Mountains   **Three Buddha Top**

The three mountains has three peaks at roughly the same level, while the three Buddha top has a higher center peak.

FIGURE 6-1 • Three Mountains and Three Buddha Top Patterns

In each case, the number three allows for sufficient testing of a resistance level before price eventually breaks lower. Each time price is repelled from a specific level, those hoping for higher prices eventually become discouraged and sell, which results in a change of price direction. Each of these patterns can be enhanced if known candlestick reversal patterns are formed at each peak.

The daily chart of KLA-Tencor Corp. (Fig. 6-2) shows an example of a three mountains pattern. In this case, resistance formed in the 68–70 price range. That is the area where those holding the stock saw maximum value. Each time price tried to break through that resistance area, sellers emerged to push price lower. Notice that on the third high, an evening star reversal pattern formed, signaling that a change in price direction was imminent.

The weekly chart of the Dow Jones Industrial Average (Fig. 6-3) shows the formation of a three Buddha top. A weekly chart has been chosen in this case to illustrate the longer term prospects of a valid three Buddha top formation. The time period shown is 2006–2008. At the top of each pattern, a spinning top formed, showing that each push higher was running out of gas. The final spinning top in December 2007 preceded one of the worst periods in stock market history.

FIGURE 6-2 • Three Mountains: KLA-Tencor Corp., Daily

Source: MetaStock

FIGURE 6-3 • Three Buddha Top: Dow Jones Industrial Average Weekly

Source: MetaStock

Three Rivers

Three rivers is similar to the triple bottom in Western technical analysis. It invokes the concept of support, which is presented in Chapter 7. Support is an area on a price chart where downtrends are stopped because buyers see value at a certain price level that induces buying. This provides support to prices, which attracts more buyers.

Another version of three rivers is the *inverted three Buddha*, which is formed by three lows, with the second one being the lowest of the three. Figure 6-4 shows examples of three rivers and inverted three Buddha bottom.

Three Rivers **Inverted Three Buddha**

The three rivers has three lows (or troughs) at roughly the same level, while the inverted three Buddha has a lower center trough.

FIGURE 6-4 • Three Rivers and Inverted Three Buddha Bottom Patterns

The daily chart of the NYSE Composite Index (Fig. 6-5) shows an example of three rivers. All three lows in the pattern were formed in the 6900–7000 range. After the third low, three white soldiers signaled that the trend had reversed.

FIGURE 6-5 • Three Rivers: NYSE Composite Index, Daily
Source: MetaStock

FIGURE 6-6 • Inverted Three Buddha Bottom: NYMEX Crude Oil Futures, Daily
Source: MetaStock

The daily chart of NYMEX Crude Oil Futures (Fig. 6-6) shows an example of an inverted three Buddha bottom pattern. Notice the alternation of white and black candles at the low point of the pattern as buyers and sellers struggled for control of price direction. The reversal was confirmed following the rising window formed after the low at point 3 was made.

Just as with the mountain patterns, the number three allows for sufficient testing of a specific price area (in this case support) before price eventually changes direction. Each time price is repelled from a specific level, selling pressure weakens, and buyers eventually emerge to take the price higher. Each of these patterns can be enhanced if known candlestick reversal patterns are formed at each low.

Three Gaps

The *three gaps* strategy is used to time entry and exit from the market. The *three upside gap strategy* (or *sanku fumiage*) says that following a third gap higher following a low, one should exit the market. Each gap is formed by short covering as traders are forced to buy back their bets against a rising market. Once the third gap higher has occurred, a top can be expected, which means that exiting long positions and adding some short positions is in order. A reversal lower is confirmed when price falls through the third (highest) upside gap. At this point, a trader should increase short positions.

FIGURE 6-7 • Three Upside Gaps: Amazon.com Inc., Daily
Source: MetaStock

The daily chart of Amazon.com Inc. (Fig. 6-7) shows an example of three upside gaps. Notice that even though the second gap was filled three weeks after it was opened, the uptrend resumed. After the third gap, long exposure should be reduced in anticipation of a top. Once the third gap is closed, one should begin adding short positions.

Three downside gaps after a top (or *sanku nage owari*) should be treated in the same manner—look for a bottom to form after the third gap lower. Once price reverses back up through the third (lowest) gap, the buying of long positions is in order. The daily chart of First Solar Inc. (Fig. 6-8) shows an example of three downside gaps. Following the third gap lower, one should begin covering short positions. Once that third gap is filled, begin adding long exposure.

Three Soldiers

The *three soldiers* strategy refers to three candles that are moving in the same direction as well as the force behind the movement. For example, the three white soldiers pattern (or *white sanpei*), covered in Chapter 4, is an example of a market that is reversing higher off of a low. This pattern shows great resolve among buyers as they enter the market causing a change in price direction. The daily chart of the iShares MSCI Emerging Markets ETF (Fig. 6-9) shows a three white soldiers pattern. Notice that the first of the three candles is actually a

FIGURE 6-8 • Three Downside Gaps: First Solar Inc., Daily
Source: MetaStock

FIGURE 6-9 • Three White Soldiers: iShares MSCI Emerging Markets ETF Daily
Source: MetaStock

bullish piercing line that signified a reversal was imminent. The three candles that formed the pattern were an unmistakable show of strength that signaled a price low was in place.

There are two variations of the three soldiers pattern, however, that can signal weakness. The first is the *advance block* pattern, which is somewhat similar but the second and third days have long lower shadows, demonstrating the onset of selling activity. The daily chart of Paychex Inc. (Fig. 6-10) shows an example of the advance block pattern. Notice how the real bodies of the candles contracted as the pattern developed, a sign of diminishing buying pressure.

The second variation is called *deliberation*, where the second day can have a long lower shadow and the third day is an indecisive spinning top or a star, indicating a change in price direction is likely near. The daily chart of the iShares Barclays 20+ Year Treasury Bond ETF (Fig. 6-11) shows an example of the deliberation pattern. The second day of the pattern has a longer lower shadow than the first, while the third day is an indecisive doji.

The three black crows pattern, or *black sanpei* (covered in Chapter 4), is the downside equivalent of the three soldiers strategy. The daily chart of the iShares Barclay's 7–10-Year Treasury Bond ETF (Fig. 6-12) shows three black crows. While this is not a textbook three black crows pattern, the thing to remember is the ominous appearance of the three descending black candles.

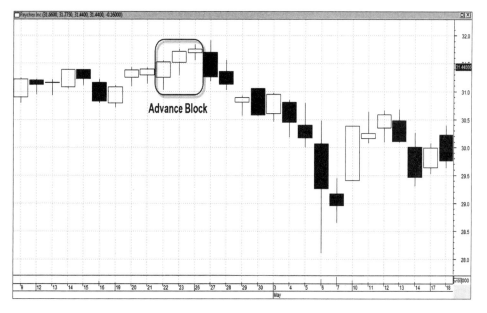

FIGURE 6-10 • Advance Block: Paychex Inc., Daily
Source: MetaStock

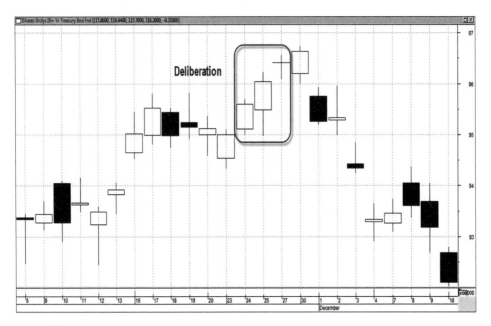

FIGURE 6-11 • Deliberation: iShares Barclays 20+ Year Treasury Bond ETF, Daily
Source: MetaStock

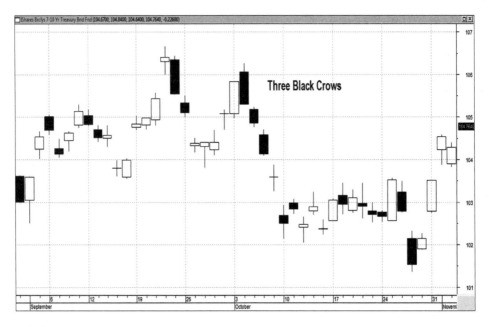

FIGURE 6-12 • Three Black Crows: iShares Barclays 7–10-Year Treasury Bond ETF, Daily
Source: MetaStock

A variation of three black crows is the *identical three crows* pattern, which consists of three descending black candles that open at the close of the previous day instead of within the real body like the standard three black crows pattern. In these patterns, the strategy uses the analogy of an unlucky crow on the top of a dead tree to compare it to a black line near the top. The terms *two-winged crow* and *three-winged crow* originated from this analogy, which was the thought process behind the naming of the three black crows pattern.

Three Methods

This strategy states simply that one must "buy, sell, and rest." This means that taking breaks from buying and selling are necessary to refresh the trader and to gain perspective on the market without having any trading capital on the line. In a rising market, the appearance of a rising three method continuation pattern (introduced in Chapter 5) shows that there will be a short rest before a further climb. The appearance of a falling three method continuation pattern (discussed in Chapter 5) shows that there will be a short rest before a further decline.

Other variations of these patterns are the *upside gap three method* and *downside gap three method* (Fig. 6-13). These were not introduced in Chapter 5 because they are contradictory to the theory behind the tasuki gap in that the gap opened between the first and second candles is completely closed on the third day, which normally increases the possibility that price will change direction. This would have been difficult to understand if presented in Chapter 5, but now that the three gaps strategy has been examined, the assumption can be made that if the gap formed is the first or second of a move, the chance of success and continuation of the trend is enhanced.

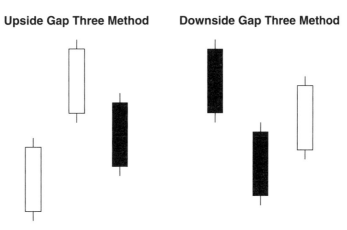

Upside Gap Three Method   **Downside Gap Three Method**

FIGURE 6-13 • Upside and Downside Gap Three Methods

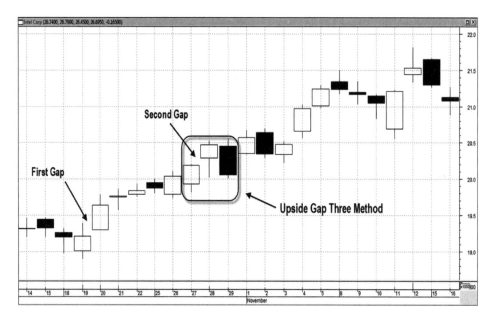

FIGURE 6-14 • Upside Gap Three Method: Intel Corp., Daily
Source: MetaStock

The daily chart of Intel Corp. (Fig. 6-14) shows an example of an upside gap three method. The pattern has five steps.

1. Price is in an uptrend.
2. The first day of the pattern forms a white candle, which confirms the trend.
3. On the second day price gaps higher at the open, and the gap between the real bodies remains open at the end of the day.
4. On the third day price forms a small gap lower at the open and then closes within the real body of the first candle, closing the gap.
5. Price opens higher the next day, forming a white candle that signifies a resumption of the trend.

It is important to notice that the gap formed in the upside gap three method is only the second gap of the overall price move higher. When we invoke the Sanku, or three gaps rule, it becomes evident that even though this gap was filled as part of the pattern, there was still room on the upside for a further advance.

The downside gap three method forms in a downtrend. The daily chart of eBay Inc. (Fig. 6-15) shows an example of the pattern.

1. Price is in a downtrend.
2. The first day of the pattern forms a black candle, which confirms the trend.
3. On the second day price gaps lower at the open, and the gap between the real bodies remains open at the end of the day.

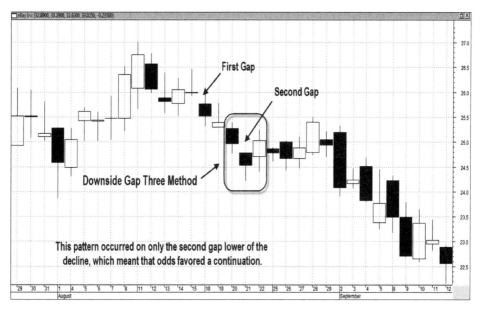

FIGURE 6-15 • Downside Gap Three Method: eBay Inc., Daily

Source: MetaStock

4. On the third day price forms a small gap higher at the open and then closes within the real body of the first candle, closing the gap.

5. Price moves sideways for five days before a long black candle signifies resumption of the downtrend.

Again, the important thing to notice is that the gap that forms in this pattern higher is only the second gap of the price move lower. Using the three gaps rule, there was still room on the downside for a further decline.

Still Struggling?

Why the number three is used in each of Sakata's strategies

The number three has been considered to have mysterious powers since premodern Japan. It is believed that a divine power lives in the number. Sayings like *sandome no shojiki*, which means "three times lucky," or the counting of "1, 2, 3" before the beginning of a race are said to have their originations in this divine power. It is the use of the number three in each of Sakata's strategies that gives the strategies an element of mysticism.

Longer Term Candle Patterns

The candle patterns covered in this section are typically longer term in nature and have longer term implications regarding price direction. These patterns should not be traded on their own individual merits, but rather their appearance can alert a trader to the possibility that meaningful change is coming. When these patterns are paired with the specific reversal or continuation patterns that were covered in Chapters 4 and 5, the chance of placing a profitable trade is enhanced. Many of the names given to the patterns covered in this section were invented by Steve Nison, who introduced them to the West.

Tower Tops and Tower Bottoms

Tower tops and *tower bottoms*, or *ohtenjyou* (Fig. 6-16), form after significant market moves and signify an abrupt change in trader sentiment. Tower reversal patterns resemble the *V* top or *V* bottom in Western technical analysis. The pattern is formed by a strong move in the direction of the trend as demonstrated by a long candle, only to be reversed a short time later by an opposite colored long candle in the opposite direction.

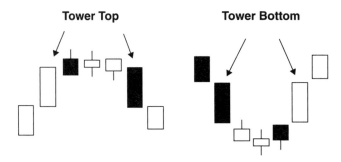

Tower Top   **Tower Bottom**

The white and black candles in these patterns form what looks like a tower.

FIGURE 6-16 • Tower Top and Tower Bottom

A *tower top* forms after a strong move higher. A long white candle forms, reinforcing the trend. Following the long white candle, price moves sideways for a time, showing trader indecision, before a long black candle forms as price reverses lower. Tower patterns are typically emotional events that can alert an astute trader that a major change in price direction is unfolding. The daily chart of the Financial Select Sector SPDR ETF (Fig. 6-17) shows an example of a tower top. The pattern develops in five stages.

1. Price is in an uptrend.
2. On the first day of the pattern, a long white candle forms, which reinforces the trend.

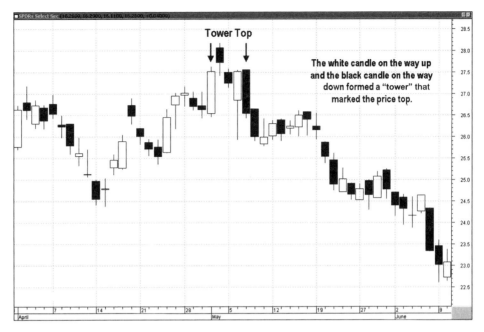

Tower Top

The white candle on the way up and the black candle on the way down formed a "tower" that marked the price top.

FIGURE 6-17 • Tower Top: Financial Select Sector SPDR ETF, Daily
Source: MetaStock

3. Over the next three days, price tries to move higher in the direction of the trend but is unable to do so.

4. On the fifth day of the pattern, a long black candle forms around the same level as the preceding long white candle.

5. That reversal signifies that sellers are gaining control, and a sharp price drop follows.

A *tower bottom* forms after a strong price decline as a long black candle is followed by a period of indecision; then a long white candle is formed, which offsets the previous long black candle. Due to the emotional event that this pattern represents, it is safe to assume that the reversal will move some distance once the reversal pattern is formed. The daily chart of Light Sweet Crude Oil (Fig. 6-18) shows an example of a tower bottom. This pattern also can be broken down into five stages.

1. Price is in a downtrend.

2. A long black candle forms, which reinforces the downtrend.

3. Price tries to move lower in the direction of the trend but is unable to do so.

4. On the fifth day of the pattern, a long white candle forms around the same level as the preceding long black candle.

5. The reversal higher shows that buyers are re-entering the market and a price rise is likely.

FIGURE 6-18 • Tower Bottom: Light Sweet Crude Oil. Daily
Source: MetaStock

An interesting point to make with regard to the crude oil chart is that two of the four candles formed between the long black and long white candles were a spinning top and a doji. Each of these on their own should have given traders pause that a change in price direction was possible. The formation of the long white candle, which reversed the effect of the long black candle, served as confirmation of the reversal suggested by the spinning top and doji.

There is nothing sacred about a period of four days between the long "tower" candles; it is just coincidence that these examples each had four days of sideways action in between. There should, however, be at least three days to show a struggle for price direction, reflecting the uncertainty that has suddenly materialized in price movement. When identifying tower tops and bottoms, it is important to remember that these patterns represent volatile periods in which price moves sharply in the direction of the trend and then reverses with an equally sharp move in the other direction. These patterns do not allow for precise trade entry but can be used as guides to determine in which direction price is likely to move over the near term.

Dumpling Tops and Fry Pan Bottoms

The *dumpling top* and *fry pan bottom,* or *nabezoko* (Fig. 6-19), are similar to the Western rounded top and bottom. They are comprised of smaller bodied candles that show indecision after a sustained price move. The color of the real bodies of the candles in this pattern is of less importance than the appearance

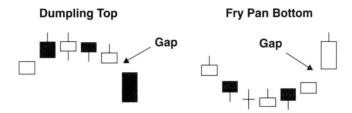

Dumpling Top   **Fry Pan Bottom**

Gap

Gap

**The color of the real bodies in the small candles
forming the top or bottom is unimportant.**

FIGURE 6-19 • Dumpling Top and Fry Pan Bottom

of the overall pattern itself. Each reversal is confirmed by a window (gap) that opens in the opposite direction of the trend.

A *dumpling top* is similar to the Western rounded top because it creates a rounded appearance as price tries to move higher, but due to a lack of buying pressure, price begins to roll over after hitting its peak. The reversal is confirmed when a falling window is opened, which signifies that sellers are taking over. The daily chart of Google Inc. (Fig. 6-20) shows an example of a dumpling top. The pattern can best be described in five pieces.

1. Price is in an uptrend as shown by the huge rising window that is opened.
2. Price continues to rise, but the trajectory begins to take on a rounded appearance as the real bodies are small.

FIGURE 6-20 • Dumpling Top: Google Inc., Daily

Source: MetaStock

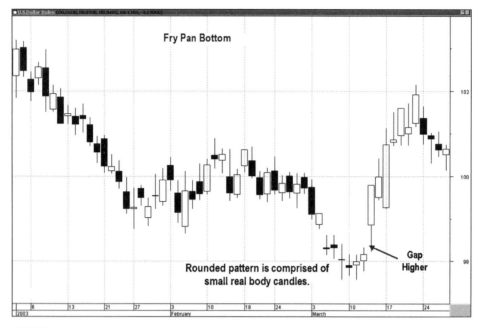

FIGURE 6-21 • Fry Pan Bottom: U.S. Dollar Index, Daily
Source: MetaStock

3. One last push higher fails.

4. A falling window is opened, which signifies that sellers are taking control.

5. Price moves sharply lower following the reversal.

A *fry pan bottom* is formed in much the same way, only it appears after a sustained decline. The daily chart of the U.S. Dollar Index (Fig. 6-21) shows an example of a fry pan bottom.

1. Price is in a downtrend.

2. Price tries to push lower, but all sellers can muster is a series of spinning tops and doji that form a rounded pattern.

3. A rising window is opened, which signifies renewed interest among buyers.

4. Price moves sharply higher from there.

Tweezer Tops and Tweezer Bottoms

Tweezer tops and *bottoms*, or *kenuki*, form with a matching pair of high prices (tweezer top) or matching lows (tweezer bottom). They resemble a pair of tweezers. In order to be a valid tweezer top or bottom, the two lines do not have to appear consecutively. In other words, this pattern can develop over a number of days. Just be mindful of the support or resistance level that is revealed by the appearance of like priced highs or lows. The ideal tweezer pattern consists of a long bodied candle followed by a second candle with a small real body that shows deterioration of trend strength. Tweezer patterns take on added significance if other reversal candle lines are a part of the pattern as it develops, such as an engulfing pattern, harami cross, and so on.

A tweezer top is formed when two or more candles reach the same high price in an uptrend, but the second candle cannot advance any further. If the second candle is a reversal candle itself (spinning top, doji, etc.), the tweezer pattern is another piece of evidence that a reversal lower in price is likely. The daily chart of the Consumer Staples Select Sector SPDR ETF (Fig. 6-22) shows a tweezer top. The pattern can be broken down in six parts.

1. Price is in an uptrend.
2. Three straight white candles form what looks to be an advance block pattern.
3. Following the third white candle, a doji forms with its high at virtually the same place as the third white candle.
4. Two straight days where price is unable to break through the high price gives bullish traders pause.
5. The next day price once again makes a run at the high but is unable to break through, further reinforcing the pattern.
6. A black candle is formed that day, showing that sellers are taking over, and price begins to move lower.

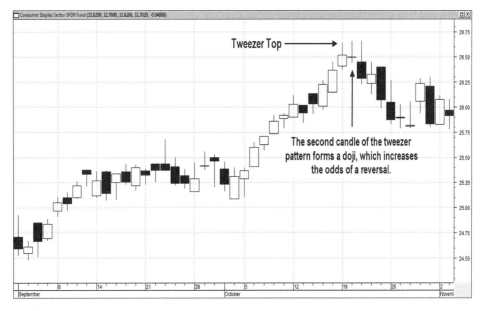

FIGURE 6-22 • Tweezer Top: Consumer Staples Select Sector SPDR ETF, Daily
Source: MetaStock

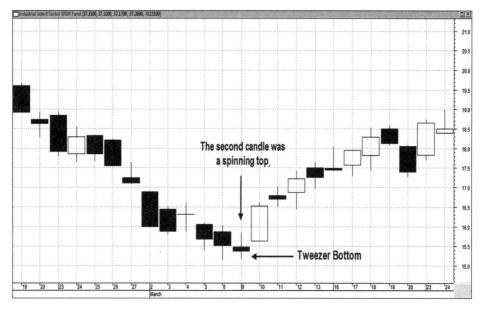

FIGURE 6-23 • Tweezer Bottom: Industrial Select Sector SPDR ETF, Daily
Source: MetaStock

A tweezer bottom forms with matching prices at a market low. The daily chart of the Industrial Select Sector SPDR ETF (Fig. 6-23) shows an example of a tweezer bottom.

1. Price is in a downtrend.
2. The real body sizes of the black candles are getting smaller as the downtrend continues.
3. The low is set with the first of the two candles in the pattern.
4. The next day the low is approached again, but price cannot break through, giving bearish traders pause.
5. On that second day a spinning top is formed, further creating doubt in the bear camp.
6. The following day a rising window is formed with a long white candle as price reverses and moves higher.

In each of these examples, the tweezers were formed on consecutive candles. Remember that is not always the case with this pattern. The candles can sometimes be days apart. Also, do not get hung up on the price having to exactly touch the previous price level for this to be a valid pattern. If the price is a tick or two off, that is also acceptable. What is important is the resistance area represented by the repelling of a further move in the direction of the trend. If one is always looking for the perfect textbook pattern, some good trading opportunities will be missed.

Gapping Plays

Gapping plays (Fig. 6-24) are patterns that develop after a strong move in the market. After such a move (whether up or down), the market takes a rest. This resting, or consolidation, period is followed by a window or gap that is opened in the direction of the trend, signaling a continuation. This pattern once again invokes the concept of the market "resting," as is the case with the *three methods* pattern discussed earlier.

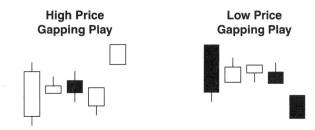

High Price Gapping Play   **Low Price Gapping Play**

**The color or type of candles in the consolidation
phase are not important. Watch for the gap
higher or lower to signal continuation.**

FIGURE 6-24 • Gapping Plays

A *high price gapping play*, or *bohtoh*, forms after a sharp advance. Its name derives from the fact that a window or gap forms at or very near a price high. A long white candle is followed by a brief period of consolidation. The formation of a rising window signals that the trend is ready to resume. The daily chart of Amazon.com, Inc. (Fig. 6-25) shows an example of a high price gapping play. The pattern develops in five steps.

1. Price is in a strong uptrend for almost three months.
2. A long white candle forms, confirming the uptrend.
3. A period of consolidation follows, which lasts for seven trading days.
4. A rising window is opened following the consolidation period, signaling that the trend is ready to resume.
5. The uptrend resumes with a series of white candles.

A *low price gapping play*, or *bohraku*, occurs in a strong downtrend. After a sustained decline, price enters a short rest period or consolidation phase. Once this period concludes, a resumption of the trend is signaled when a falling window or downside gap is opened. The daily chart of the Select Sector Financial SPDR ETF (Fig. 6-26) shows an example of a low price gapping play. Look for five stages in this pattern.

1. Price is in a strong downtrend.
2. A long black candle forms, which confirms the downtrend.

FIGURE 6-25 • High Price Gapping Play: Amazon.com, Inc., Daily

Source: MetaStock

FIGURE 6-26 • Low Price Gapping Play: Select Sector Financial SPDR ETF, Daily

Source: MetaStock

3. A period of consolidation follows, which lasts for three trading days.

4. A falling window is opened following the consolidation period, signaling the trend is ready to resume.

5. The downtrend resumes with a series of black candles.

The appearance of gapping plays in trending markets can be a sign that the trend is ready to resume with a vengeance. However, one must always be aware of the number of gaps that have appeared before the appearance of the gapping play. If two or more gaps have already appeared prior to this one in the trend, caution is advised as the market is due for a reversal of some sort. Volume can also be used to help determine whether a gap is signaling a continuation or the end of a price move. Gaps will be studied in Chapter 7, while volume analysis will be covered in Chapter 9.

Eight New Price Lines

The principle of *eight new price lines*, or *shinne hatte*, is governed by the philosophy that one should take profits after eight new price highs are set. These do not have to be eight days in a row, but eight new highs in an upward price move. The daily chart of Apple Inc. (Fig. 6-27) shows two examples of eight new price lines within a larger degree price move. Notice how after each instance of eight new highs, there was a reaction as price moved lower.

FIGURE 6-27 • Eight New Price Lines: Apple Inc., Daily

Source: MetaStock

Some literature suggests that profits be taken after 10, or even 13, new price highs. If traders wait that long, they risk having to sit through some rather sharp reactions as Fig. 6-27 illustrates. It is best to at least begin to take profits after eight new highs. One way to do that is to take off 80 percent of long exposure and let the other 20 percent ride in the event that the move makes 10 or more new highs. The point is that some sort of action is advised following eight new highs.

Summary

- Sakata's strategies were part of 160 trading rules written by Munehisa Honma.
- The number three is a major part of these strategies.
- Honma did not use candlestick charts, but these patterns form the basis of candlestick pattern analysis.
- Sakata's strategies are broader patterns that forewarn of longer term market reversals.
- Three mountains and three Buddha top involve three price peaks to form a top.
- Three rivers and inverted three Buddha involve three price lows to form a bottom.
- Three gaps are used to time entry and exit from the market.
- The three soldiers strategy refers to three candles moving in the same direction and the force behind the movement.
- Three methods means "buy, sell, and rest" and signals that one should take a break from the market periodically.
- Tower tops and bottoms are emotion events that are similar to *V* tops and bottoms in Western technical analysis.
- Dumpling tops and fry pan bottoms are similar to the rounded top and bottom in Western technical analysis.
- Tweezer tops and bottoms are so named because they resemble a pair of tweezers as price reverses at the same level.
- Gapping plays develop after a strong move in the market followed by a period of rest.
- Eight new price lines signal when one should take action to lock in profits.

QUIZ

1. **Which of Sakata's strategies means "buy, sell, and rest"?**
    A. Three gaps
    B. Three methods
    C. Three soldiers
    D. Three rivers

2. **Which pattern resembles a *V*-type reversal in Western technical analysis?**
    A. Dumpling top
    B. Gapping play
    C. Tower top
    D. None of the above

3. **Which candle pattern encourages taking profits at a specific point?**
    A. Three soldiers
    B. Fry pan bottom
    C. Eight new price lines
    D. All of the above

4. **Who wrote Sakata's strategies?**
    A. Munehisa Honma
    B. Sansiko Sakata
    C. William Shakespeare
    D. Vladimir Lenin

5. **A tweezer pattern must always form on two consecutive candles.**
    A. True
    B. False

6. **Which pattern most closely resembles the Western head and shoulders top?**
    A. Dumpling top or bottom
    B. Three Buddha top
    C. Tower top or bottom
    D. None of the above

7. **Which reversal pattern closes a gap on the third day before the trend resumes?**
    A. Upside gap three methods
    B. Tasuki gap
    C. Deliberation
    D. Advance block

8. **The three black crows pattern is the upside equivalent of the three soldiers strategy.**
    A. True
    B. False

9. **What type of reversal pattern is shown in the chart below?**

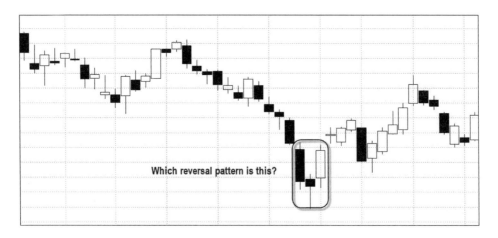

Which reversal pattern is this?

   A. Fry pan bottom
   B. Three river bottom
   C. Inverted three Buddha
   D. Tower bottom

10. **Which reversal pattern is a derivative of three soldiers?**
   A. Deliberation
   B. Advance block
   C. Three black crows
   D. All of the above

UPPER
SHADOW

OPEN

REAL
BODY

LOWER
SHADOW

CLOSE

HAMMER

Chapter *7*

Basic Technical Analysis

Thus far we have examined the basics of candlestick charting and its origins, reversal patterns, continuation patterns, and the psychology behind these patterns. Now we will examine the framework for applying the mechanics of candlestick charting that we have learned. As the next step, we will add trend analysis, support and resistance, retracement levels, and a closer look at gaps to our trading arsenal. These are all components of modern-day Western technical analysis that, when combined with candlestick charting techniques, can generate a much deeper understanding of the position of the market and what it is likely to do next. Notice the word *likely*. In trading, there are no guarantees. Technical analysis does not guarantee trading success, it is merely a tool to tilt the odds of accurate market analysis in your favor.

The purpose of this chapter is to acquaint you with some basic principles of technical analysis to give you more tools to use in your trading. When these tools are combined with candle pattern analysis, a synergy is created that does not exist when these tools are used separately. The topics discussed here merely scratch the surface of technical analysis, but these concepts work well with candle pattern analysis.

CHAPTER OBJECTIVES

In this chapter, you will

- Learn basic technical analysis
- Gain an understanding of methods of trend identification
- Identify and understand support and resistance
- Understand internal and external retracement levels
- Explore types of gaps and their meanings
- Combine candle patterns with technical analysis for more effective trading

Technical analysis is simply the study of price movement. It constantly analyzes the supply/demand relationship for the market as a whole, individual stocks, or commodities. As traders see value in a particular stock or commodity, its price tends to rise over time, until fair value is reached or it becomes overvalued. At that point the price direction, or trend, will likely change, and price will either move sideways or begin to fall as a new value level is sought. Conversely, if a particular stock or commodity is seen as having decreasing value, its price will fall until it reaches a level that entices buyers to enter the market and offset the supply of shares or contracts for sale.

Trends

A *trend* is the tendency of price to move in a specific direction over time. For example, when price makes higher highs and higher lows, an *uptrend* is in force, while a series of lower highs and lower lows is defined as a *downtrend*. Identifying the trend is very important when trading as it tells a trader in which direction the market current is flowing. Recall from Chapter 1 that the market current is comprised of the collective will of traders. If good value is perceived in the market and traders want to bid prices higher, the current (or trend) is up. If traders perceive poor value and want to sell their shares, the trend (or current) is down. Just as trying to swim against a river current is in many cases a fruitless endeavor, so is trading against the flow of capital in the market. There are three basic methods to determine the trend:

1. Visual inspection of the chart (higher highs and higher lows or lower highs and lower lows)
2. Moving averages
3. Trend lines

When attempting to identify the trend of price movement, the first topic a trader should address is what time frame he or she is interested in. For example, in the daily chart of Exxon Mobil Corp. (Fig. 7-1), notice the different trends

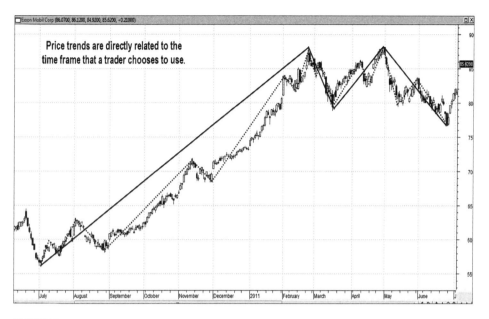

FIGURE 7-1 • Price Trends: Exxon Mobil Corp., Daily
Source: MetaStock

that can coexist on the same price plot. The solid lines represent the longer term price trend, while the dotted lines represent shorter term price trends. This chart illustrates that smaller degree price trends can exist within larger degree trends. The shorter term trends take on their own structure and periodically move against the larger degree trend.

   This means that if you were to ask a day trader and a position trader (who can hold positions for weeks or months) what the trend of the market is, you may get two conflicting answers, but each would be correct since they are viewing the market within their own trading time frame. Just to prove that point further, take a look at the chart of Exxon Mobil Corp. in Fig. 7-2. The price plot consists of 10-minute bars. In other words, it takes 39 bars to make up an entire trading day, or one bar on a daily price chart. Notice again the larger degree trend that can be broken down into smaller degree trends. In intra-day trading, a larger degree trend may last a day or two as compared with those that can last weeks or months in the daily time frame.

Moving Averages in Trends

Another way to determine price trend is by using a moving average of price. A moving average shows the average price of a security or commodity over a specified time period. Moving averages are used to smooth out price fluctuations, which can interfere with proper assessment of the trend. There are many different varieties of moving averages such as simple, exponential, weighted,

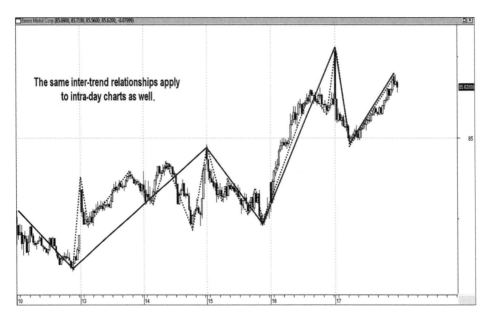

FIGURE 7-2 • Price Trends: Exxon Mobil Corp.—Ten-Minute Bars
Source: MetaStock

triangular, and so on. The two styles used most frequently are simple and exponential. An exponential moving average gives more weight to recent price action, while a simple moving average gives equal weight to each day used in its calculation. Either method can be plotted by any competent charting package with just a couple of mouse clicks. We will use the simple moving average.

A simple moving average is the easiest to compute. In order to compute a 20-day simple moving average, add the previous 20 days of closing prices and divide by 20. When the next day's closing price is known, re-total the most recent 20 days and divide that number by 20. This causes the 21st day prior to fall out of the calculation, causing the 20-day average or price to change, or "move," with the latest price data. The daily chart of The Coca-Cola Company (Fig. 7-3) shows an example of a 20-day simple moving average, which is on the edge between a short or intermediate time frame.

The direction of the moving average is used to discern the price trend. When the moving average is moving higher, the 20-day price trend is up, and when the moving average is moving lower, the 20-day price trend is down. There are times when the moving average is moving higher, but price closes below it, and vice versa. During these times, the trend is said to be neutral since the moving average moving in one direction has been contradicted by price closing on the other side of the moving average. Sometimes these situations are short-term anomalies as price quickly jumps back above or below the moving average to reestablish the trend. In other cases, this type of action is an early indication of a developing change in trend.

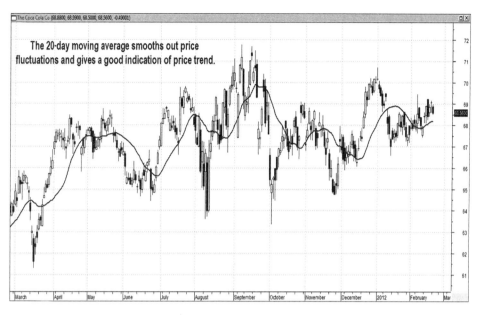

FIGURE 7-3 • 20-Day Moving Average: The Coca-Cola Company, Daily
Source: MetaStock

Another good use of moving averages is to use certain price behavior patterns as times to anticipate short-term change in price, which can help an astute trader lock in profits or try to scalp short-term trades against the prevailing trend. Trying to scalp trades against the trend (putting on a short position in an uptrend) carries more risk because the trader is fighting the flow of the market, but it can be done by more seasoned traders. The daily chart of Coca-Cola is once again presented (Fig. 7-4), but this time we have added an indicator in the bottom pane that reflects the percentage that the closing price is above or below the 20-day moving average. This is a very simple momentum indicator to compute:

$$[(\text{Closing price} / \text{20-day moving average of closing prices}) - 1] \times 100$$

The theory behind using an indicator like this is that price tends to move in a rhythm or pattern depending on the security or commodity traded. For example, some stocks make wider swings than others, but each one has certain characteristics that can be exploited with price analysis. In this case, a visual inspection of the time period plotted on the chart shows that when price closes approximately 4 percent above or below the 20-day moving average, price tends to change direction. Now this does not guarantee a full trend reversal, but sound trading opportunities can present themselves; or the more conservative trader may choose to lock in profits by selling long positions when price is 4 percent above the moving average, or cover short positions when the price is

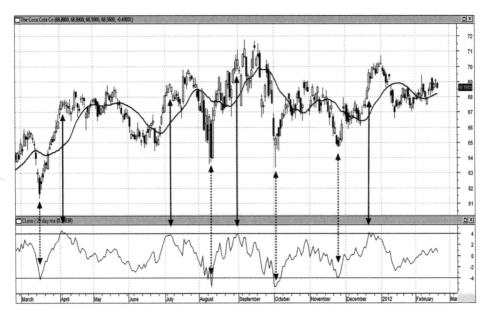

FIGURE 7-4 • 20-Day Moving Average with Indicator: The Coca-Cola Company, Daily
Source: MetaStock

4 percent below the moving average. This methodology is a very simple way of exploiting volatility extremes. As volatility reverts back to its mean, or average, these trades have a higher chance for success.

By using this indicator coupled with the candlestick reversal patterns previously identified, a trader can pinpoint high probability turning points. Think about the synergy here. This methodology combines candlesticks (which reveal the mindset of traders) with the natural rhythm of the market (pinpointing situations where price is likely to reverse). With that said, regardless of how much sense a trade makes and how sound the thought process is behind it, stop loss orders should always be used because the markets are notorious for making us all look foolish at one time or another.

One final feature to highlight regarding this simple yet effective indicator is to point out that it can also reveal divergences or situations where price movement is running out of gas. This concept will be discussed in more detail in Chapter 8, but for now, let's define it as price making higher highs while the indicator makes lower highs. What this means is that as price moves higher, it is not separating itself as far from its 20-day moving average as it had on earlier pushes higher. This loss of upside momentum is a red flag that the buying pressure that pushed price higher in the past is weakening, which leaves price vulnerable to moves in the opposite direction. Figure 7-5 shows the same daily chart of Coca-Cola, but this time the middle of the chart is slightly enlarged so you can see the candlestick pattern and indicator divergence at the September 16, 2011, high.

FIGURE 7-5 • 20-Day Moving Average with Indicator Divergence: The Coca-Cola Company, Daily
Source: MetaStock

Notice as price moved higher in early September, the indicator made a series of lower highs (the dotted lines). On September 16, buyers produced one last gasp effort to push price higher, which resulted in the formation of an evening star pattern. As price reversed lower, the selling intensified, which made for a great trading opportunity.

This technique can be used with any length moving average to help a trader uncover trading opportunities in any time frame. Suggested settings for moving average lengths are 5–20 days for short-term trading, 21–60 days for intermediate trading, and 61 days or more for long-term trading.

One final note regarding moving averages is the concept of *lag*. The more days of data are used to construct a moving average, the slower the moving average will react to changes in price direction. This concept is illustrated in the daily chart of Bank of America Corp. (Fig. 7-6).

Notice that the 20-day moving average (dashed line) is much more reactive to changes in price, while the 100-day moving average is much smoother. While the 20-day moving average will provide earlier signals regarding a change in price trend, it is also prone to more false signals, or *whipsaws*. At point A, the 20-day moving average began to move higher to signal a change in the 20-day trend. Shortly thereafter, however, the downtrend resumed with a vengeance as price pushed to new lows. At point B, the 20-day moving average turned higher, and it turned out that this was a bona fide trend reversal. The 100-day moving average did not turn higher until point C, about one month later. So while the

FIGURE 7-6 • 20-Day and 100-Day Moving Averages: Bank of America Corp., Daily
Source: MetaStock

longer term moving average did not give a false signal like the shorter term moving average at point A, a price was paid by waiting an entire month to get into the market. Which moving average length is better? That is solely up to the individual trader. Knowing the time frame you want to trade and sticking to it will allow you to select a trusted companion by using the proper length moving average. Moving averages are also good areas for support and resistance in trending markets. That concept will be presented later in this chapter.

Trend Lines—Identifying the Trend

A trend line is a line that shows the trend of the market by connecting successive highs or lows. While most traders simply draw trend lines by connecting low points in an uptrend or high points in a downtrend, trend lines are much more versatile than that and can be used to project potential price turning points in the future.

The daily chart of the SPDR S&P Retail ETF (Fig. 7-7) shows an example of "classic" trend lines that are drawn by many chartists. Are these lines valid? Absolutely. Do they tell the *whole* story of where price may change direction? Not really. Line A connects the tops of descending highs, which shows resistance that is acting as a barrier to price advances. Line B connects the bottoms of ascending lows, which shows support that is helping price to reverse higher. This forms a nice triangle that when broken to the upside shows that the previous uptrend is ready to continue.

FIGURE 7-7 • Classic Trend Lines: SPDR S&P Retail ETF, Daily
Source: MetaStock

Now let's take a look at the chart one more time, only with additional trend lines added. Figure 7-8 still has the original trend lines labeled A and B. Now lines C, D, and E have been added with each labeled near its point of origin. This type of trend line is also referred to as a support/resistance line. Yes, it is following the overall trend, but what is more important is how price reacts when it touches this line. Line C connects the February and June lows, line D connects the May high with what I call a "split" just off of the July high (more on that in a minute), and line E connects the June low with the October high. When these lines are projected forward, future areas of potential price reactions are given. This is like knowing in advance where price reactions are likely to occur. When potential reversal zones on a chart are combined with candlestick reversal patterns, trades have an increased chance for profitability. Notice at point F how two lines converged, and as price ran into that combination, it reversed and moved lower. A combination of two or more trend lines concurrently coming into contact with price is a very powerful indication that price will change direction, at least temporarily.

As for the "split" I spoke of on line D, this illustrates a principle for trend line drawing that is much easier to visualize on candlestick charts. If you look at the origin of line D, it was drawn off of the May high. It is connected, however, to the bottom of a real body on a candle that was formed *after* price made its high. Why? Because following the formation of that candle, a falling window opened after which two attempts were made to climb back into the real body of that candle, forming in-neck lines with that candle. That is strong resistance and is a price area that must be considered as valid when drawing trend lines and connecting price

FIGURE 7-8 • More Trend Lines: SPDR S&P Retail ETF, Daily
Source: MetaStock

points. Using candlestick charting allows a chartist to see these situations more clearly than would a person using simple bar charts. Trend lines should typically originate from meaningful highs and lows, but sometimes the more subtle areas of price inflection make better connection points off of those highs and lows. Looking more deeply into price movement can allow for the drawing of meaningful trend lines that are missed by those that simply connect highs and lows.

Parallel trend lines drawn on a chart make up a *channel* or a sloping boundary that is likely to contain prices. The daily chart of the Industrial Select Sector SPDR ETF (Fig. 7-9) shows an example of equidistant trend lines that act as support or resistance when encountered.

The original trend line was drawn off of the bottom of the real body of the candle that marked the October low. The second, or middle, line was drawn along the support area that formed as price moved higher at point B. From there, a parallel line was projected higher from the high at point C. Notice how each line acted as support or resistance at one time or another during the uptrend. These are also areas where price inflection points can be expected.

When a trend line is violated, a signal is given that a change in price trend is likely. Another point to remember is that the longer the trend line and the more touches it has, the more meaning it has. For example, a trend line that has been in place over a three-month period and has been touched many times by price is more meaningful than a trend line that has existed for three weeks and has been touched a couple of times by price.

FIGURE 7-9 • Channels: Industrial Select Sector SPDR ETF, Daily
Source: MetaStock

Support and Resistance

Support and *resistance* are terms given to price zones on a chart that tend to prevent price from falling further (support) or from rising further (resistance). These are terms that we have touched on earlier, but now a deeper explanation is in order. There is nothing magical about support and resistance levels. These are levels at which traders change their opinions regarding the valuation of a security or commodity.

In our discussion of trends, we established that uptrends are driven by demand being a stronger force than the number of shares or contracts for sale. For downtrends, demand is weak, which means the supply of shares or contracts for sale is not readily absorbed, which tends to drive prices lower. Price will continue to fall until there is sufficient demand from buyers to absorb the supply, thus stabilizing price.

Support/resistance areas or zones come in the following forms:

- Horizontal lines or bands
- Trend lines
- Moving averages
- Retracement levels

Horizontal Lines or Bands

A support zone is a place on a chart where price has declined and turned higher in the past. These are areas where buyers have found sufficient value to increase demand, which offsets the supply of shares or contracts being brought to the market for sale. As price declines into a zone that has provided support in the past, it is reasonable to expect demand to increase at the same level. There are no guarantees that this will occur, however, so make sure that buyers are indeed entering the market before buying simply because a price has encountered a support level. This means waiting for confirmation of any candle reversal patterns that may appear. If a support area is broken, that is a bearish development and *what was once support now becomes resistance*, which will impede future advances at that level.

The daily chart of Barrick Gold (Fig. 7-10) shows an example of a support zone on a chart. In June, October, and December 2011, price declined into the 43–45 range, and each time traders saw sufficient value to begin buying shares to offset the supply of shares offered for sale. As buyers went to work, the short-term dynamics changed and the price began to rise. The support area was originally established in June on the first reversal higher from the 43–45 area, so it was reasonable for price to at least bounce the next time it encountered that level. Look closely at the October and December lows. What evidence of reversals higher do you see? In October there are two hammers with very long lower shadows. In December a bullish piercing line was formed in the support area. Each of these instances provided evidence that buyers were becoming more active, which caused price to rise.

FIGURE 7-10 • Support Area: Barrick Gold Corp., Daily
Source: MetaStock

The concept of broken support becoming resistance is easy to grasp if you look at it from a psychological aspect. Those that initiated new positions using the previous support level as a guide now become sellers as price reaches the broken support level from below. The reason for this is they recognize that the market dynamics have changed and are happy to get out as close to breakeven on the trade as possible. The daily chart of the Financial Select Sector SPDR ETF (Fig. 7-11) illustrates this concept. Notice first how the 32.00–32.50 price zone provides support for declining prices on the left side of the chart. After price broke down through the support zone in early November, two later attempts to climb back above support were turned away. There is no better evidence of a change in trader sentiment than the candles that were formed as price touched this zone. On the left side where it was support, numerous long white candles were formed. Following the November break, two later encounters with the same price zone from below saw the formation of long black candles, indicating that sellers had indeed taken control of price direction. This shows the synergy of methodologies as the combination of support and resistance along with the deeper insight given by candlestick charting can give a trader an edge in these situations.

Resistance is a price level or range at which more shares come on the market for sale, which keeps price from advancing further. Resistance is formed when price reaches a level that causes traders to think that the security or commodity is fully valued. As price approaches that level, sellers intensify their efforts to get what they believe is fair value for their shares or contracts. In many cases it

FIGURE 7-11 • Broken Support Now Resistance: Financial Select Sector SPDR ETF, Daily
Source: MetaStock

FIGURE 7-12 • Resistance Area: Terra Nitrogen Co., Daily
Source: MetaStock

takes multiple efforts to break through resistance as the number of shares for sale need to be absorbed repeatedly by willing buyers. The daily chart of Terra Nitrogen Co. (Fig. 7-12) shows an example of a clearly defined resistance area.

The resistance area is quite well defined with a horizontal line drawn across the 26 price level on the chart. Resistance was first established in November 2005 (on the left side of the chart). That instance as well as three others that followed were all identified with long black candles as price retreated from the 26 level due to intense selling pressure. These instances are marked with black arrows. Price finally broke though that resistance level in October 2006 as two long white candles formed, which showed that buyers had absorbed the shares for sale at the 26 level and demand was sufficient to push price higher.

Following the break of resistance, price then mildly retreated to the 26 level as what was once resistance is now support. This is also a phenomenon known as *testing* a prior resistance area as price will retreat to "tag" the area before continuing its move higher. The same type of testing occurs in break-downs under support and is shown in Fig. 7-11 as price broke down through support then rallied up and touched the prior support area before continuing lower.

Another use of candlestick charts is in finding support and resistance areas by adding horizontal lines that run through areas that touch the real bodies of multiple candles. The daily chart of the S&P 500 Index (Fig. 7-13) shows how this technique can help a trader identify levels that are important to the market.

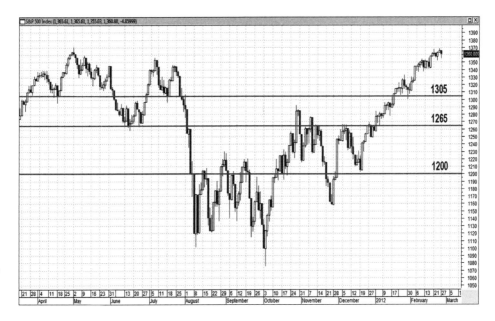

FIGURE 7-13 • Horizontal Zones: S&P 500 Index, Daily

Source: MetaStock

The three price levels identified were 1305, 1265, and 1200. Notice how the 1305 level had multiple touches from April to July 2011 on the left side of the chart. Price either reversed direction after touching this line, or if the line was broken, price movement accelerated.

The 1265 level was touched by clusters of candles in June and December 2011. Also note the long real bodies of the candles that formed as price traded through the 1265 level multiple times from October to November 2011. The long real bodies demonstrate elevated trader emotion, which makes this level meaningful to the market as buyers and sellers battle to gain control of price direction. Finally, the 1200 level shows a large number of real bodies as price moved back and forth through that level from August to November 2011. Price also found support just above the 1200 level before beginning its strong rally to kick off the 2012 trading year.

At the time of this writing, the markets are well overdue for a pullback, but the powers that be (the U.S. Federal Reserve and the European Central Bank) will not let natural market forces take over as these powers continue to flood the markets with cheap cash, which is finding its way into the equity markets. That means that when a pullback does occur, it will be sharp and likely sudden, as the natural forces of supply and demand can only be distorted for so long before they reassert themselves with a vengeance. Identifying levels such as these by using past price action of candlesticks can help traders anticipate where price reactions may occur as the previous price trend reverses.

Trend Lines

By their very construction, trend lines are drawn by connecting points at which price reacted or changed direction in the past. These qualities give trend lines the dual distinction of being able to identify trends as well as support/resistance levels. The daily chart of the Walt Disney Co. (Fig. 7-14) shows an example of an uptrend line and its support/resistance characteristics. The example we will use here is for the intermediate or long-term trader.

The trend line is constructed by connecting the lows of the real bodies of the candles at points A and B (the lower left corner of the chart). This gives a rough estimation of where price reactions can occur in the future. When drawing trend lines, don't get hung up on creating the perfect trend line that catches every single touch of the line. These lines are to give a trader an area or zone where a price reaction should occur. This is not about nailing it down to the exact price tick. As the trend line is carried forward, notice how price found support at the line at point C after forming its March 2011 high. After price made its high in March 2011, it reversed lower and traded down to the trend line at point C. Upon encountering the trend line, price reversed sharply higher as shown by the long lower shadow of the candle that touched the line. Price then mounted one last charge at the prior high but was unable to break through as it met strong resistance. Price subsequently rolled over and encountered the trend line one more time at point D. It briefly found support at point D but

FIGURE 7-14 • Trend Line Support/Resistance: The Walt Disney Co., Daily
Source: MetaStock

eventually broke through the trend line. Notice that price twice tried to break back above the violated trend line but was unable to do so. This is yet another example of what was once support is now resistance.

Moving Averages

Earlier in this chapter, we discussed moving averages for assessing trend, but they also show support/resistance characteristics. As moving averages "move" with price, they tend to form support areas in uptrends and resistance areas in downtrends. The daily chart of Ryder Systems, Inc. (Fig. 7-15) shows an example of a 20-day moving average providing support and resistance as price moves higher or lower. The shaded areas show where the moving average acted as support or resistance to price movement. If these encounters with the moving average are combined with candle reversal or continuation patterns, profitable trading opportunities can present themselves.

FIGURE 7-15 • 20-Day Moving Average Support/Resistance: Ryder Systems Inc., Daily
Source: MetaStock

Retracement Levels

A *retracement* is a price movement in the opposite direction of the previous trend. Retracements are also referred to as *pullbacks* or *corrections* in trading jargon as traders of the previous trend exit the market to lock in profits. A retracement level is a level at which price is expected to find support as price retraces from a prior high or resistance as price retraces from a prior low. Retracement levels are computed by taking percentages of the difference between the high and low of the previous price swing. There are two types of retracement levels, *internal* and *external*.

The most popular method for computing retracement levels among traders today is the Fibonacci series. Fibonacci numbers were developed by Leonard of Pisa and consist of the numbers 1, 2, 3, 5, 8, 13, 21, 34, 55, 89, 144, 233 and so on. Each number in the series is the sum of the previous two numbers. For example, 2+3=5, 3+5=8, 5+8=13, and so on. The most important point to make regarding this series is that each successive number is 1.618 times the previous number. For example, $34 \times 1.618 = 55, 55 \times 1.618 = 89$, and so on. If you want to know the number that is the second one back from the current number in the series, multiply that number by 0.382. For example, $144 \times 0.382 = 55$. If you want to know the third number back, multiply by 0.236. In that case, $144 \times 0.236 = 34$. If you want to find the number four places back, multiply by 0.146: $144 \times .146 = 21$. You can play with the rest of the numbers to test this out if you are so inclined.

The reciprocal of 1.618 (0.618) is also a very important number in the series. Whenever these numbers are added, subtracted, multiplied, or divided, the resulting number will always yield a Fibonacci ratio. For example, $1.618 \times 0.618 = 0.382, 0.618 \times 0.382 = 0.236$, or $0.236 \times 0.618 = 0.146$. Subtraction also yields Fibonacci ratios as well: $0.618 - 0.382 = 0.236, 0.382 - 0.236 = 0.146$, and so on. External retracement levels are computed by multiplying. For example, $1.618 \times 1.618 = 2.618$ and $2.618 \times 1.618 = 4.236$.

Internal retracements occur between prior highs and lows. The most important internal retracement levels to consider are the Fibonacci levels of .382 and .618. The 50 percent retracement level (.50) is always an important level as in many cases, price reacts at the halfway point of the prior move. The daily chart of FedEx Corp. (Fig. 7-16) shows an example of internal retracements.

There are five areas labeled on the charts as A through E. The distance between the high price (A) and the low price (B) for the downtrend are used as the measuring points for the retracement levels. Once the levels are plotted, notice the price reactions as price encounters these levels on the bounce higher. First at point C, price gapped through the 38.2 percent retracement level by forming a rising window. Next, at point D, price reversed lower in its first encounter with the 61.8 percent retracement level. After price sold off and chopped around for about six weeks, it once again reversed higher and tried repeatedly to break through the 61.8 percent retracement level as shown by the action at point E. Price continued to move higher once it penetrated the 61.8 percent retracement level, but the struggle that occurred at that level was a testimony to the importance of that level. The reactions at each of the price levels once again illustrates the concepts of support and resistance. For example, following the initial penetration of the 38.2 percent level at point C, price twice

FIGURE 7-16 • Internal Retracement Levels: FedEx Corp., Daily
Source: MetaStock

encountered that level later and used it as support to stop declines and reverse price higher.

The daily chart of United Parcel Service Inc. (Fig. 7-17) shows a good example of using internal retracement levels to trade. The high and low of the range are marked as A and B, respectively. Following the low at point B, price rebounded and made a run at the 38.2 percent retracement level, which is labeled point C. Notice that price never quite touched the 38.2 percent retracement level before a hanging man appeared, which is a bearish reversal signal. The fact that price did not even make it to what looked to be a natural resistance level gave an indication that the market was weak and more selling needed to occur before price could rebound. A short trade could have been entered on the candle following the hanging man as price closed below the real body of the hanging man. A protective buy stop should have been placed just above the 38.2 percent retracement level.

Price then declined to point D, where an inverted hammer formed, which was followed two candles later buy a long white candle, which should have been a signal to lock in profits. After price reversed higher, it managed to rally to the 50 percent retracement level at point E where a shooting star formed. The combination of a natural resistance level with a powerful candle reversal pattern was a great place to initiate another trade. A short trade could have been placed on the candle following the shooting star as price closed lower. As far as stop placement goes, use the higher of the high of the upper shadow

FIGURE 7-17 • Internal Retracement Levels: United Parcel Service Inc., Daily
Source: MetaStock

or the 50 percent retracement level. That is what we did on the previous trade at the 38.2 percent level. This provides a little extra room to prevent a stop loss from being hit before price reverses lower. In this case, the top of the shooting star was higher than the retracement level, so the top of the shooting star was used.

External retracement levels are levels that retrace outside the previous range. In other words, if a retracement was calculated from high to low, price exceeds the prior high and continues upward. Using these external ratios can give very accurate levels at which one can expect a change in price direction. Again, there is nothing magical about these levels, but when candle reversal patterns appear near them, that is more evidence that tilts the odds in favor of a reversal. The best external levels to use are 127.2 percent, 161.8 percent, 261.8 percent, and 423.6 percent.

The daily chart of Amgen Inc. (Fig. 7-18) shows an example of external retracement levels. After price declined from May to August 2011, the range was established. In order for the external retracement levels to come into play, price must first eclipse the May high, or make a greater than 100 percent retracement of the May–August decline. Once price cleared that hurdle, the external retracements could be drawn. Again, encountering these levels does not guarantee a change in trend, it merely adds more weight to a candle reversal pattern should one form. Notice the reaction that price had at point A as it encountered the 127.2 percent retracement level. If you can strain your eyes

FIGURE 7-18 • External Retracement Levels: Amgen Inc., Daily

Source: MetaStock

to see it, a shooting star formed, which signaled that a reaction of some sort was beginning. That reaction did not last long, however, as the uptrend resumed shortly thereafter. This is another example where using a stop price would save one from unnecessary losses. Once it reached point B at the 161.8 percent retracement level in late January 2012, a doji formed, signaling that another price reaction was unfolding. The encounter with the 161.8 percent retracement at point B provided a better trading opportunity.

Retracement levels can have even more meaning when levels from multiple ranges cluster around the same area on a chart. These clusters increase the odds of a price reversal, especially when combined with a valid candle reversal pattern. The daily chart of FLIR Systems Inc. (Fig. 7-19) shows an example of two separate retracement levels coming into play at virtually the same price level.

The first retracement range is off of the price decline from A to B. The second retracement range is off of the price decline from C to D. Notice how the 38.2 percent retracement of the A–B range coincides almost exactly with the 61.8 percent retracement level of the C–D range (both are circled on the chart). This overlap causes very strong resistance as the chart demonstrates. Price turned lower on the first two attempts to break through that synergistic level as marked by the two downward pointing arrows. After successfully breaking through on the third try, price retreated to that level once again and used it as support before continuing its advance (marked by the upward pointing arrow). This invokes the principle that what was once resistance is now support.

FIGURE 7-19 • Retracement Cluster: FLIR Systems Inc., Daily

Source: MetaStock

 Still Struggling?

Support and resistance reflect supply/demand dynamics.

Those that do not use technical analysis seem to think that there is a bunch of hocus pocus behind these very important levels. The key to remembering their importance is to understand that they reflect shifts in the supply/demand dynamics of the market. Support is where buyers see good value so they enter the market to buy shares. Resistance is a level at which sellers see peak value so they exit the market by selling their shares. The breaking of these levels shows that previous perceptions of valuation have changed, which causes price to look for a new level to equalize supply and demand. This ties in with trend analysis as well. When support or resistance is broken, typically a new trend is born.

Gaps

Gaps or windows in candlestick jargon are one and the same. We have already discussed gaps or windows in Chapters 5 and 6. Since this chapter is on Western technical analysis, we will refer to them as gaps here and look at the different types of gaps and the psychology behind them. As stated in Chapter 5, a gap is an open spot or a break on a price chart that forms between the close of one day and the opening of the next. Gaps are typically emotional events that are driven by news stories, earnings reports, economic reports, changes in management, and so on that cause trader sentiment to escalate in either a positive or negative direction. This change in sentiment can cause an imbalance of buy or sell orders, and the opening price adjusts to a new level based on the type and number of orders. Whenever a gap forms, traders must pay attention as these shifts in sentiment can provide profitable trading opportunities. There are four classifications of gaps:

- Common gaps
- Breakaway gaps
- Runaway gaps
- Exhaustion gaps

Common Gaps

A *common gap* is usually an uneventful gap. One way it can be formed is by a thinly traded stock going ex-dividend. Common gaps also occur in range-bound, choppy markets that have little meaning. The thinner the trading volume in a stock, commodity, or ETF, the more likely a common gap will form. The best way to look at a common gap is that if price did not gap through significant support/resistance or form on a noticeable jump in volume, then it is likely a common gap. The daily chart of CSX Corp. (Fig. 7-20) shows common gaps.

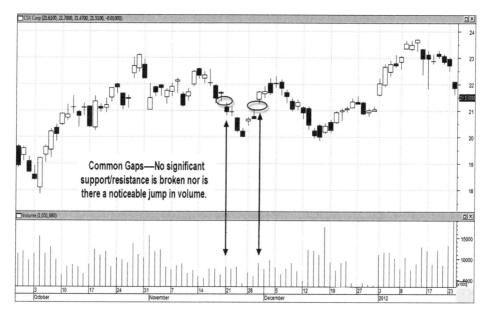

FIGURE 7-20 • Common Gaps: CSX Corp, Daily
Source: MetaStock

Breakaway Gaps

A *breakaway gap* occurs when price breaks out of a trading range or a period of consolidation. These gaps are usually accompanied by a large increase in volume as those holding positions in the opposite direction of the breakout are forced to sell or cover those positions. Breakaway gaps signal that a significant change in sentiment has taken place and that the price movement in the direction of the gap is expected to continue. This also means that the open gap should be an area of future price support (for upside gaps) or resistance (for downside gaps). The daily chart of Amazon.com Inc. (Fig. 7-21) shows an example of a breakaway gap.

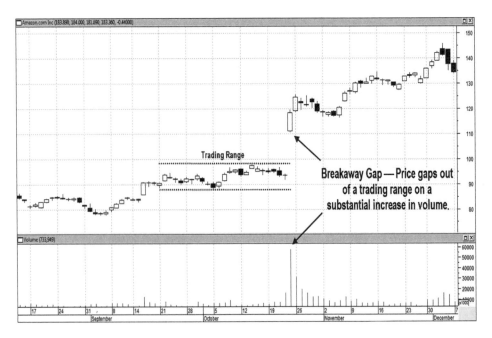

FIGURE 7-21 • Breakaway Gap: Amazon.com Inc., Daily

Source: MetaStock

Runaway Gaps

A *runaway gap* forms in an already trending market. The trend increases in intensity due to either a new piece of news or because those that had been waiting for a trend pullback to jump on board never got the chance. In any case, volume increases, which shows that trader interest has intensified. The trend continues after formation of the gap, which means that this type of gap usually remains open for a while. The daily chart of Apple Inc. (Fig. 7-22) shows a runaway gap.

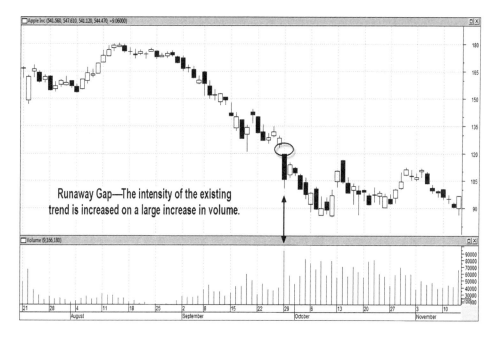

FIGURE 7-22 • Runaway Gap: Apple Inc., Daily

Source: MetaStock

Exhaustion Gaps

An *exhaustion gap* forms at the end of a strong price move. Exhaustion gaps can be mistaken for runaway gaps, so one must be careful to look for exceptionally high volume that is caused by almost panic buying (uptrend) or selling (downtrend) by those that are afraid they will miss what is sure to be another sharp move in the direction of the trend. Exhaustion gaps are easily spotted on price charts in hindsight and mark areas of extraordinary greed in uptrends or fear in downtrends. Great care must be taken when trading around these events as the elevated fear or greed causes wild swings in price volatility, or the magnitude of price movements. The daily chart of Southwest Airlines Co. (Fig. 7-23) shows an exhaustion gap. Notice the large downside gap accompanied by a huge amount of volume. That gap marked the bottom of the downtrend as virtually everyone who was able to sell sold their shares in what was likely a state of panic.

As discussed in Chapter 5, gaps, or windows, also mark significant support and resistance levels that can be used for sound stop loss order placement when entering a trade. Remember, too, that the filling of a gap can signal a change in price direction and must be noted.

FIGURE 7-23 • Exhaustion Gap: Southwest Airlines Co., Daily
Source: MetaStock

Summary

- Technical analysis is the study of price movement.
- Technical analysis helps a trader determine what price is likely to do.
- The supply-and-demand dynamics of the market are what help determine the trend.
- Identifying the price trend can help a trader identify good trading opportunities.
- Visual inspection of the chart, trend lines, and moving averages are used to identify the trend.
- The direction of the trend depends on the time frame that the trader uses.
- Support and resistance are areas where price can be expected to reverse direction as it has done in the past.
- Support and resistance levels come in the form of horizontal price areas, trend lines, moving averages, and retracement levels.
- A gap is an open spot or a break on a price chart that forms between the close of one day and the opening of the next.
- Gaps reflect high-emotion events that are triggered by news stories, economic reports, earnings reports, and so on.
- Gaps come in four types: common, breakaway, runaway, and exhaustion.

QUIZ

1. Technical analysis is the study of price movement.
   A. True
   B. False

2. Technical analysis can help a trader be certain what price will do next.
   A. True
   B. False

3. Trend is the tendency of price to move in a specific direction over time.
   A. True
   B. False

4. Which method is used to assess the price trend?
   A. Support and resistance
   B. Horizontal lines or bands
   C. Moving averages
   D. None of the above

5. Which method is used to assess support and resistance?
   A. Horizontal lines or bands
   B. Trend lines
   C. Moving averages
   D. All of the above

6. If price breaks down through support, what does the broken support then become?
   A. Useless
   B. Enhanced support
   C. Resistance
   D. A bottom

7. What is one concept to be aware of when choosing a moving average length?
   A. Trend line fit
   B. The certainty of support/resistance areas
   C. Reversal probability
   D. Lag

8. Trend lines should only be drawn touching extreme price highs and lows.
   A. True
   B. False

9. Gaps on a price chart reveal periods of high trader emotion.
   A. True
   B. False

10. **Which if the following is not a valid type of gap?**
    A. Breakaway
    B. Common
    C. Explosion
    D. Runaway

Chapter **8**

Candlesticks and Momentum Indicators

Now that we know the extra layer of insight that candlestick charting can provide, let's go a step further and show the synergy that can be achieved by combining candlesticks with momentum indicators. A momentum indicator is used to measure the *rate*, or *velocity*, at which price moves up or down. Momentum indicators can be computed over short-term, intermediate, or long-term time frames, which means they can be used in virtually any time frame that a trader prefers. These versatile indicators can be used in conjunction with candle patterns to spot trades that have higher probability for success than if each method were used on its own.

CHAPTER OBJECTIVES

In this chapter, you will

- Understand the basic uses of momentum indicators
- Know the strengths and weaknesses of momentum indicators
- Understand the difference between banded and centered oscillators
- Understand the computation and characteristics of the most widely used momentum indicators
- Learn what to consider when developing your own momentum indicators
- Combine momentum indicators with candle patterns for more effective trading

Momentum Indicator Basics

Before we proceed, however, it is necessary to caution new traders against thinking that these indicators are more than they actually are. Momentum indicators are not fail-safe—they can be fooled and give bad signals to traders on occasion. Again, that is why stop loss orders should be used on every trade. Momentum indicators should be used as a portion of a *weight of the evidence* trading methodology that can tilt the odds of success in a trader's favor. For example, if the momentum indicator is flashing a signal that price is at such a level that the odds of a price reversal have increased, is there a candlestick pattern saying the same thing? Is there a support or resistance area nearby that can reinforce the likelihood of price behaving in a manner the trader expects?

Momentum indicators are used to measure the rate of advance or decline in the market—or velocity of price movement—so they are great for determining the health of trend momentum, which can give a trader valuable clues as to whether a change in the price trend may be on the way. As momentum begins to slow in the direction of the trend, the trader should take no action unless price itself *confirms* a reversal. This principle is best described with an analogy: if a person is driving a car at 35 mph and takes his or her foot off of the gas, the car will begin to decelerate—*it does not immediately begin to move in reverse.* The concept is the same with momentum indicators. When price momentum begins to slow, it may actually take some time for price to reverse direction. This is why looking for reversal candle patterns when momentum begins to slow is a great way to get an early jump on these situations. As candle patterns develop, the psychology of the traders moving the market is on display for astute traders to see, which means that price action should eventually confirm what the momentum indicator is telling you. If momentum begins to slow and there is no candle pattern to trade off of, simply do nothing. We are only interested in trades that are signaled by more than one tool at our disposal.

Momentum indicators may be plotted on different scales and be computed differently, but all essentially have three main uses:

1. Displaying *overbought* and *oversold* levels—or levels from which price momentum is likely to slow or change direction
2. Revealing differences between price movement and its momentum (divergences)
3. Analyzing the overall momentum trend

Oscillators

The first four momentum indicators presented in this chapter are all forms of oscillators because they oscillate between overbought and oversold levels (banded oscillators) or they move above and below a center line (centered oscillators).

Regardless of the look of any particular indicator, remember that they serve the three purposes just listed. Also, just as with moving averages, the longer the period used to compute a momentum indicator, the smoother it will be.

With banded oscillators, this means that the indicator is less likely to reach overbought and oversold levels as momentum indicators computed over a shorter time frame. This will become apparent as you experiment with momentum indicators of different time lengths. The examples of momentum indicators here should be used as a foundation to develop a basic understanding of their functions and how they can be used. It is not the goal of this chapter to show you every possible trading situation with these indicators. It will be up to you to get comfortable with the indicator of your choice and make it fit with the trading time frame you desire. In this chapter we will explore the construction of the indicators, the reasoning behind them, and their uses. We will then bring candlestick patterns back into the picture and show how the two can be combined to enhance the probability of placing profitable trades. At the end of this chapter, I will introduce a momentum indicator that I developed that is effective when combined with candlestick charting.

MACD

The *MACD* indicator is a centered oscillator that consists of a single line that is the difference between two moving averages of price. This single line is plotted with its own moving average, known as the "signal line." Crosses of the signal line by the MACD are typically used as trading signals. In order to understand the MACD, let's quickly review the moving average oscillator indicator presented in Chapter 7, as the evolution of that concept forms the basis for the MACD.

Recall that in Chapter 7 two uses for the moving average oscillator were shown—first it was used to show when price was stretched from its moving average, which resulted in trading opportunities as the volatility between price and its moving average reverted back to its mean (overbought and oversold levels). In addition, the moving average oscillator was used to show periods when the indicator diverged from the price trend. In other words, price made a higher high but the indicator made a lower high in an uptrend, or price made a lower low and the indicator made a higher low in a downtrend.

Yet another way to use this indicator is by using zero line crossovers as buy or sell signals. For example, when price closes above its 20-day moving average, the indicator will be above the zero line; when price closes below its 20-day moving average, the indicator will be in negative territory, or below the zero line. While the concept is sound, the actual implementation of the signals can cause whipsaws as the price sometimes crosses above and below its moving average in rapid succession. The daily chart of American Express Co. (Fig. 8-1) illustrates this issue. Notice that on the left side of the chart clear signals were given, but toward the middle of the chart, three straight periods of whipsaw signals

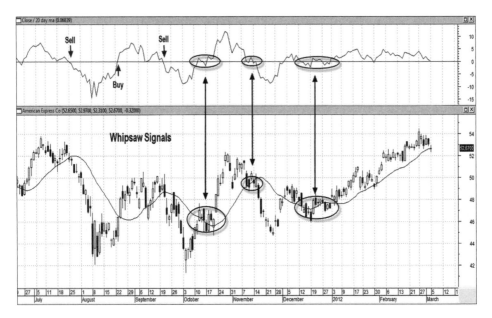

FIGURE 8-1 • 20-Day Moving Average Oscillator Whipsaws: American Express Co., Daily
Source: MetaStock

occurred (circled). This can be a problem, so we must adjust our indicator accordingly, which forms the foundation for the MACD indicator.

In order to smooth out the whipsaw periods, a short-term moving average is used instead of the daily closing price for comparison to the longer term moving average (in this case 20 days). Let's plot the indicator now with a 5-day moving average substituted for the closing price compared to the 20-day moving average and note the differences (Fig. 8-2). The result is a much smoother line with fewer whipsaw signals, but also note that due to the smoother five-day moving average, the signals come somewhat later (angled arrows). That is always the trade-off when using momentum indicators. Efforts to reduce whipsaw signals result in later (but usually more reliable) signals. The daily chart of American Express (Fig. 8-2) has the 5-/20-day oscillator plotted above the original moving average oscillator. A five-day moving average has also been added to the price plot as a dashed line. Notice how the first two whipsaw signals have been removed. The third whipsaw was not totally eliminated, but it was reduced from three whipsaws down to one.

This brings us now to the MACD indicator itself. The MACD is composed of two exponential moving averages, which means that the moving averages are more sensitive to recent price movements compared to the simple moving averages we have used thus far that give an equal weighting to each day in the computation. The exponential moving average itself can be easily plotted with any competent charting package, but for those who want to calculate the values

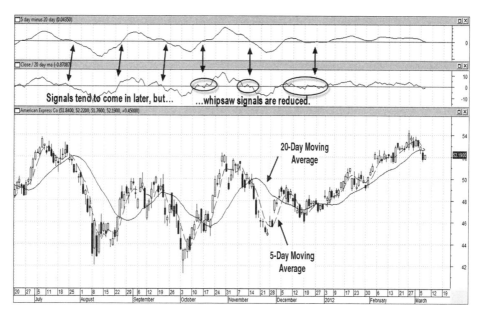

FIGURE 8-2 • Moving Average Oscillator Smoothed: American Express Co., Daily
Source: MetaStock

for themselves, a great explanation on its calculation can be found in *Technical Analysis from A to Z* by Steven Achelis.

The typical default values for an MACD indicator is the difference between 12-period and 26-period exponential moving averages, with a 9-period signal line. The MACD indicator is plotted on the same chart of American Express (Fig. 8-3). Notice how smooth the movement is in the MACD, which makes it a valuable tool for assessing the overall trend. The MACD is a versatile indicator that can be combined with candlesticks to produce some great trading opportunities.

One of the methods used to trade the MACD is using crossovers of the signal line as triggers to enter and exit the market. I am not a big fan of that methodology for two reasons. First, in spite of its smoother appearance, there are still whipsaw periods with regard to the crossovers that can cause trader losses as the signals switch from buy to sell and back again. Those types of whipsaw signals are even more costly in a slower moving indicator like the MACD because by the time the MACD reacts and gets synched up with price movement, price is already well on its way to moving in the other direction. The second reason I don't like using signal line crossovers as trade triggers is that the timing of the crossovers does not always coincide with a valid candle reversal pattern. In some cases, a price reversal may occur that is followed later by a MACD crossover, while in other cases the MACD begins to change direction as price momentum wanes while the price trend itself continues for a bit longer. These issues will become evident as we look at a few examples.

The MACD moves in a smooth, trendlike fashion.

FIGURE 8-3 · MACD: American Express Co., Daily
Source: MetaStock

The daily chart of Caterpillar Inc. (Fig. 8-4) shows an example of the MACD and how it can alert a trader to a higher probability of success when trading with candle patterns. The first instance shows a positive divergence where price made a lower low than the previous low, but the MACD made a higher low. This shows latent buying pressure, which in many cases results in a reversal of price direction. Notice that at the divergent low a bullish piercing line formed. That reversal pattern combined with the positive divergence on the MACD meant that the trader had an increased chance for success because the momentum indicator verified that Caterpillar was in a higher probability state for a price reversal.

The next two trading examples were evident by the nonconfirmation of price reaching its previous high as the MACD made two successive lower highs. The first instance showed that the MACD was already moving lower as price reached its previous high. The formation of an evening star pattern at that point was an indication that price was going to follow momentum lower as indicated by the weakening MACD. The next opportunity saw price make it back up to the same high level yet again, while the MACD made an even lower high. While the candle pattern was not as concise as in the first two examples, three straight small bodied black candles demonstrated that trend was weakening. Once price traded below the low of the final white candle into the high, a short trade could have been entered.

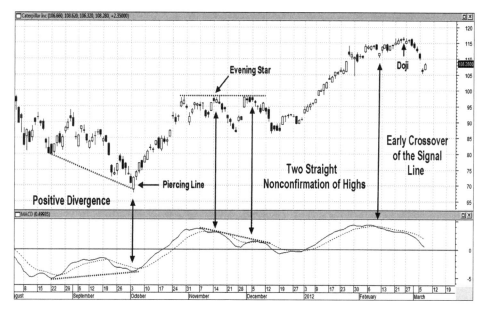

FIGURE 8-4 • MACD Trades: Caterpillar Inc., Daily

Source: MetaStock

Finally, take a look at the far right side of the chart. This is an example of why I am wary of trading off of MACD signal line crossovers. The double-sided arrow shows where the MACD crossed below its signal line, which to some traders is a signal to put on a short position. The MACD showed that momentum was definitely waning as it started moving lower, but price advanced for another *nine days* following the downside cross. Anyone who went short based solely on the crossover was sitting on some tough losses before the price trend eventually changed. Notice during the final push higher that not one valid reversal pattern had formed until the doji on the ninth day following the crossover, which was confirmed by a hard reversal lower.

Another example of a good use for the MACD is to verify the existing trend and bolster confidence in candlestick continuation patterns. The daily chart of Exxon Mobil Corp. (Fig. 8-5) shows an example of using the MACD to verify that a separating lines pattern is likely to be a success. Notice that price set a low in November, and as it began moving higher, the MACD also started its uptrend. Price then paused in December as it moved sideways for five days before forming the separating lines pattern. One look at the MACD showed no divergences as the MACD also remained firmly above its zero line, which verified that the shorter term 12-day moving average was above the longer term 26-day moving average. With positive momentum still behind price movement, the odds increased for a successful resolution of the separating lines pattern to the upside.

FIGURE 8-5 • MACD Continuation: Exxon Mobil Corp., Daily
Source: MetaStock

The MACD is a great indicator for verifying the price trend. If divergences appear along with a candlestick reversal pattern, the odds increase that a reversal in the price trend will develop. If the MACD verifies the strength of the trend and a continuation pattern appears, the odds for a successful resumption of the trend increase. Remember also that you do not have to use the default 12- and 26-day settings for the MACD that come with most charting packages. Feel free to experiment with different combinations of moving average lengths to form the indicator that works best for you.

Rate of Change

Rate of change (ROC) is a simple indicator that is effective yet very easy to calculate. Its simple method of calculation can be misleading to those who believe the more complex an indicator's calculation is, the more effective the indicator is. Nothing could be further from the truth. The ROC is elegant in its simplicity but is also a very effective tool to show not only trend strength, but also trend divergences.

The ROC is calculated by computing the difference between today's closing price and the closing price n periods ago. The ROC can be calculated two ways. The first is subtraction: $ROC = C - Cn$, where C is today's closing price and Cn is the closing price n periods ago. The second and more robust method is division: $ROC = [(C/Cn) - 1] \times 100$, where C is today's closing price and Cn

is the closing price *n* periods ago. The division method provides a more accurate look at how price moved on a percentage basis. For example, consider a $2 price move on a $5 stock and a $50 stock. By using the subtraction method, each situation would yield a result of 2 (the difference between today's closing price and the closing price *n* days ago). So if price moved from $5 to $7, by doing the math, we would get a rate of change of 2 since 7 − 5 = 2. Using the subtraction method on the $50 dollar stock would yield the same result. If price advanced to $52, ROC = 52 − 50, or 2.

The division method, however, provides much different results. On a price move from 5 to 7, the ROC computes to 40 as ROC = [(7 / 5) − 1] × 100. This means that price made a 40 percent move over the period measured by the ROC. A $2 move on a $50 stock would yield an ROC value of 4, meaning the price advanced 4 percent. It is obvious which move was more meaningful. Using the subtraction method there would be no difference, while using the division method would show a great difference in the significance of the price movement.

The ROC is a centered oscillator, which means that readings above the zero line show positive price momentum while readings below the zero line show negative price momentum. Even though the ROC is centered, it can also show trend strength by examining the areas where it changes direction. This concept is known as *range shift*. The daily chart of Ameriprise Financial Inc. (Fig. 8-6) illustrates this point. Below the price plot is a 20-day ROC. Notice how the ROC tends to bottom at the zero line and spend much more time above the

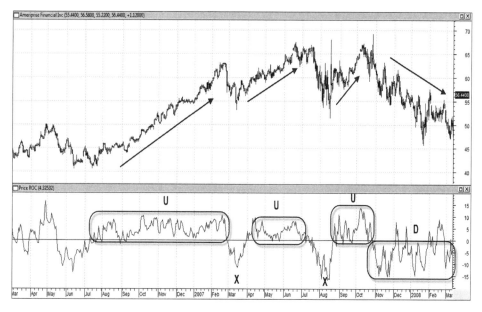

FIGURE 8-6 • ROC Trend: Ameriprise Financial Inc., Daily
Source: MetaStock

zero line in uptrends (marked as *U* on the chart) and how the ROC tends to top at the zero line and spend much more time below the zero line in down-trends (marked with a *D*). The bottoming at or near zero in uptrends shows positive price momentum, while topping at or near the zero line in downtrends shows negative price momentum. The two areas marked with an *X* are classi-fied as deep corrections since the ROC plunged deep into negative territory but quickly recovered to reflect the uptrends that followed. Remember, a trend is the tendency of price to move in a certain direction *over time*, so deep plunges below the zero line do not count as downtrends. A downtrend would be estab-lished in the ROC if it had topped at or near the zero line two or more times. While there is no substitute for looking directly at the price plot for trend determination, ROC can be used as a rough guide to assess the trend direction and its strength.

For an example of how the ROC can be used to spot high percentage trading opportunities in the intermediate term, look at the daily chart of Ameriprise in Fig. 8-7. The chart is once again plotted with a 20-day ROC below price. The example shown is at the October 2011 low. Price had been in a downtrend since May. That period is not shown so that we can zoom in on the area where the trade occurred. Notice as price broke down to what would be its final low in October that the ROC was actually making a higher low, flashing a positive divergence. This showed latent buying strength in the market, which meant the odds had increased that the downtrend would reverse. Blindly trading

FIGURE 8-7 • 20-Day ROC Trade: Ameriprise Financial Inc., Daily
Source: MetaStock

divergences is not wise, however, as they don't always result in timely reversals. What is needed in this situation is something else to tell a trader that it is time to move on the divergence. That extra piece of evidence appeared in the form of a piercing line reversal pattern. Once the reversal was confirmed by the piercing line pattern, the trade could be entered with a higher level of confidence as the change in sentiment reflected by the piercing line was reinforced by the positive momentum divergence.

When more active traders use the ROC indicator in conjunction with candlesticks, one option is to use a shorter time frame such as a 10-day ROC, given the short-term effect that candle reversal patterns can have. That does not mean that candlestick trades cannot turn into longer term trades, but a shorter term ROC can better match the time frame of more active trading.

The daily chart of Plum Creek Timber Co. (Fig. 8-8) shows a trading example using a 10-day ROC. Notice first that since the early June low on the left side of the chart (point A), price had been in an uptrend as categorized by higher highs and higher lows on its way to its first price high in late June at point B, which formed a resistance level as price retreated into a shallow pullback. Price then made one more push higher into resistance at point C where a shooting star formed. While all of this price drama was unfolding, the ROC was telling its own story in the lower pane. Notice how the ROC confirmed the price movement into the June high, but then as price rallied into the early July high at resistance (point C), the ROC was noticeably lower and had in fact

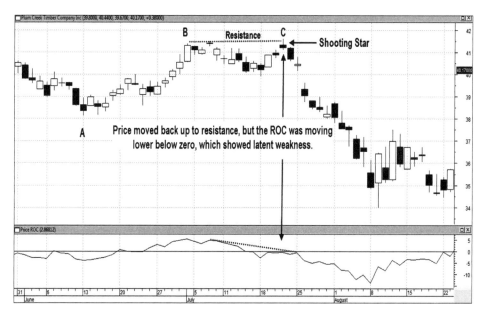

FIGURE 8-8 • 10-Day ROC Trade: Plum Creek Timber Co., Daily

Source: MetaStock

slipped below the zero line, showing negative momentum. In other words momentum had turned south before price, which really reinforced the reversal implications of the shooting star pattern. The weight of the evidence in this case was a shooting star reversal pattern that formed at resistance with the 10-day ROC making a lower high below the zero line. All of those elements coming together increased the odds of making a successful trade.

Another use of the ROC indicator is to measure the momentum trend. Just as with price, trend lines can be used on momentum indicators. There is a school of thought that trend lines should only be used on price plots because that is where the rubber meets the road and where buyers increase their activity as price encounters support or resistance. I disagree, however. Using trend lines on momentum indicators can also give a trader a picture of when buyers are increasing their buying or selling activity—a necessary component of price movement. Sometimes momentum can build before price actually begins to move, which gives a great indication that a strong price move is ready to begin. Also, momentum trend line breaks can be great coincident indicators with candlesticks. Momentum trend breaks coupled with candle reversal patterns can be a powerful combination to verify that a change in price and momentum trend is developing concurrently.

The daily chart of Apollo Group Inc. (Fig. 8-9) shows how trend lines can be used on the ROC in conjunction with candlesticks. The chart is plotted with a 10-day ROC in the bottom pane. Price was in a downtrend from July to September 2011 (left side of the chart). The pattern of lower highs

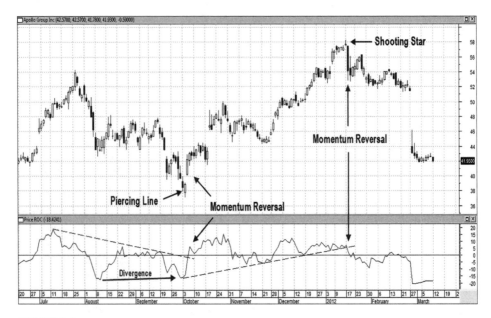

FIGURE 8-9 • ROC Trends: Apollo Group Inc., Daily
Source: MetaStock

confirmed that price momentum was in synch with price movement. As price made what turned out to be its final low at the end of September, a slight bullish divergence occurred as the ROC made a slightly higher low while price made a lower low. The next day a bullish piercing line pattern formed, alerting traders that a reversal in price was likely. When price closed higher on the third day of the pattern by opening a rising window, the ROC also confirmed the reversal in the price momentum trend by breaking up through its own downtrend line. The bullish divergence combined with the piercing line pattern followed by a trend line break in the ROC provided the weight of the evidence that tilted the odds of a successful trade into positive territory.

Following that reversal, price then embarked on a new uptrend—confirmed by the positive momentum trend in the ROC. As price moved higher into January 2012, momentum was waning as the ROC was making a series of lower highs. The ROC lows, however, continued their upward movement, so a trend line connecting the lows was valid. In cases like these, momentum can begin to weaken, but that does not mean that price is ready to reverse, just like the example of the car that decelerates but doesn't go into reverse. By connecting the lows, we are looking for a definitive move lower to confirm a reversal in the trend of price momentum. Sure enough a shooting star pattern formed in early 2012, and as price confirmed the reversal with the long black candle just after the shooting star, price momentum reversed also as price plunged sharply lower.

Stochastic Oscillator

A *stochastic oscillator* shows where the latest close is in relation to the price range over a desired period. Introduced by George Lane, it is a favorite among traders due to its standardized scale and ease of computation.

The theory behind the stochastic oscillator is that price closes closer to the upper end of its trading range in up-trending markets and closer to the bottom end of its trading range in down-trending markets. As price trends mature, closes near the extreme of the range become less common, which alerts a trader that a change in price direction may be imminent.

Construction of the stochastic consists of two lines called %K and %D. The data needed for %K are the current close with the highest and lowest prices for the period being computed. For example, in order to compute a five-period %K, the current close, highest price, and lowest price over the last five periods are needed. The formula is $\%K = 100 \times [(C - Ln)/(Hn - Ln)]$, where Ln is the lowest low over the last n periods and Hn is the highest high over the last n periods.

The %D is a smoothed version of %K and is derived as a moving average of %K. In many cases, %D is a three-period moving average of %K, but it is perfectly acceptable to set %D to another length if you wish. Just remember, the slower the %D line, the slower the crossovers between %K and %D will be.

In many charting packages, the stochastic oscillator is plotted as a *slow stochastic*. A slow stochastic is a smoothed version of %K paired with a %D that is usually a three-period smoothing of an already smoothed %K. The setting for a five-period slow stochastic would be 5, 3, 3 with the 5 representing the number of periods used in the %K calculation, the first 3 representing the %K smoothing, and the second 3 representing the %D or further three-period smoothing of the already smoothed %K. This means that %D is a double smoothed version of the original (or raw) %K value. The reason for using the slow stochastic is that it is less volatile and gives more reliable signals than the "raw" or unsmoothed version of %K.

The stochastic is categorized as a *banded oscillator* because it has consistent levels that act as overbought and oversold levels. The default values in many charting packages are 80 for overbought and 20 for oversold. The range for overbought and oversold levels tends to shift, however, depending on the direction and strength of the price trend. Also, the crossover of %D by %K is used for trading signals, but one must be careful using these signals because even the smoothed, slow stochastic can produce whipsaw trading signals. Whipsaws are less prevalent in stochastic oscillators computed over 10 periods and higher, but in reducing the prevalence of whipsaws by using these slightly longer time frames, a trader can introduce the element of lag. The frequency of whipsaw signals can also be lessened by combining crossover signals with candle reversal patterns.

The stochastic is a great indicator to use at turning points in the market. One method is to confirm candle reversal patterns with the position of the %K and %D lines. While I am not a fan of using %K and %D crossovers as the sole signals for making trades, the concept of shifting price momentum combined with actual price reversals is quite appealing. The daily chart of Home Depot (Fig. 8-10) shows an example of combining candle reversal patterns with a slow stochastic (5, 3, 3).

On the left side of the chart, price declined into point A, where a long black candle followed by an inverted hammer gave a signal that a reversal higher was possible. Notice in the bottom pane that the stochastic oscillator had been in oversold territory (below the 20 line) and that the %K line had crossed above the %D line *before* price actually made its low. The long black candle merely caused the %K to touch %D one more time, but following the formation of the inverted hammer, price momentum or velocity had already turned to the upside. The long white candle that followed the inverted hammer confirmed the reversal.

Following the low at point A, price advanced before hitting resistance in early July and then retreated to point B. This is an interesting situation. Notice as price retreated into B and the stochastic reached oversold territory (below 20), the pullback was rather shallow, typically an indication of a strong price advance. Once again—as was the case at the point A low—%K had already crossed above

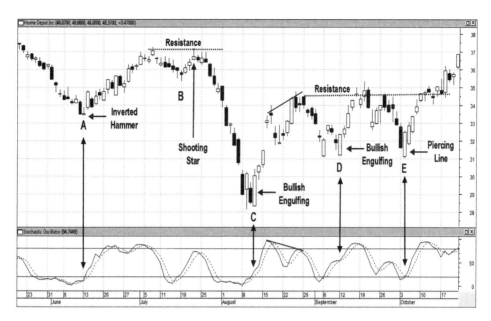

FIGURE 8-10 • Stochastic Trades: Home Depot Inc., Daily
Source: MetaStock

%D, showing a shift in price momentum or velocity. As price formed the low at point B, it was not that far below the recent high posted in early July, which meant that a resistance zone would be coming into play very soon should price mount another rally. There would be nothing wrong with taking a trade here following the hammer at the point B low, but those looking for longer term opportunities would be better off waiting for resolution of the resistance zone. Nimble traders who can pay close attention to their positions would be perfectly fine taking this trade. As price rebounded and moved higher out of the point B low, the three days following were small bodied white candles with the third day forming a shooting star right at resistance. This was a signal for more active traders who may have entered trades at point B to consider closing the trade.

Sure enough, price declined sharply into the low at point C. Notice once again that as price made its way to its final low, the stochastic oscillator reached oversold territory indicating that a change in price momentum was likely near. %K crossed above %D, showing a shift in price momentum even before the bullish engulfing pattern was formed. Once the bullish engulfing pattern at point C was confirmed, price momentum had already shifted, indicating that any new position taken there would in effect have the wind at its back.

Following the high between points C and D, price declined, and just to the left of point D, you will notice a spinning top was followed by a long white candle that formed an in-neck line. This is normally a continuation pattern, so it was not a valid buy signal. However if you had chosen to buy following the rising window that formed the next day, your stop should have been placed below the low of the long white candle that formed the in-neck line. This would have been a tempting trading opportunity since price momentum had already turned higher (%K was over %D). Placing the protective stop below the low of the white candle would have kept you in the game as the great trading opportunity at point D developed. At point D, a bullish engulfing pattern formed, which is a much stronger buy signal than the previous in-neck line. Also notice that the stochastic had been trending higher for a few days as it was already at mid-range levels. There was much latent strength behind this bullish engulfing pattern, but one concern remained. Remember at point B where there was recent price resistance looming overhead? The same issue was present at the point D low as the reactionary high just before the point D low was not very far away. Again, those looking for a longer term trading opportunity may not have been comfortable taking this trade with resistance only a couple of points away, which speaks to your own individual trading style. If you are willing to take more frequent, shorter term trades, then make the trade. If you prefer to hold for longer periods and look for larger gains, then this is one more consideration you must address.

After the point D low, price was not able to break through the resistance level just discussed, so price once again moved lower into point E as %K slipped into oversold territory. This time a bullish piercing line formed, and on the formation of the pattern, the stochastic oscillator showed positive price momentum as %K crossed above %D. Once again, however, the same resistance area loomed that turned prices lower between points C and D and points D and E. One other point to make here is that the lows at points D and E both came around the 31 level, which showed support among buyers as two powerful reversal patterns formed. This showed strong conviction at that level, which may be enough to push price through this tough overhead resistance level. Longer term traders had the same consideration, but this time the added support at 31 is another weight of the evidence piece that could tilt the scales in favor of taking the trade. Following the low at point E, buying pressure was sufficient to break through the resistance level in the 34–35 range to push prices sharply higher.

The solid line over price and the stochastic oscillator between the point C and point D lows illustrates a negative divergence situation that was shown by the stochastic. As price pushed out to a slightly higher high, the stochastic made a lower high. This was not highlighted during our discussion, which concentrated on long side entries only. This is another situation where aggressive traders playing both sides of the market could have initiated a short position as price formed a falling window off of the high. There was no solid reversal pattern, however, except for the spinning top two days before the gap lower. So while the opportunity was not overly compelling, the stochastic divergence alerted the trader from a momentum standpoint that a short trade opportunity may have been possible.

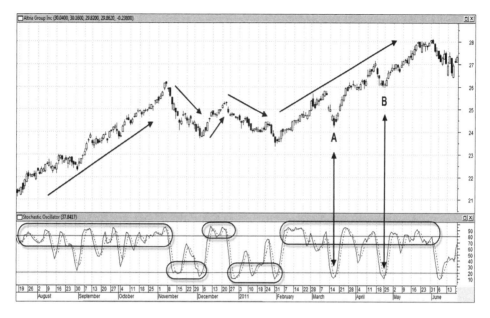

FIGURE 8-11 • Stochastic Trends: Altria Group Inc., Daily
Source: MetaStock

The previous example shows how the stochastic can be used to help with swing trades, or trades that occur with the ebb and flow of the market. There are also other uses for the stochastic, such as assessing the price trend and its strength. The daily chart of Altria Group Inc. (Fig. 8-11) shows an example of a 5, 3, 3 stochastic and how it can confirm the price trend. Each period of advancing or declining prices is shown with arrows while the corresponding time period is circled below on the plot of the stochastic. Notice that during periods of rising prices, the stochastic tends to stay near the top of the range, while in periods of falling prices, it tends to cluster near the bottom. This veri-fies the theory behind the development of the stochastic oscillator. During periods of rising prices, closing prices tend to be near the top of the range, while in periods of falling prices, closing prices tend to be near the bottom of the range.

There are two points on the chart marked A and B. These represent great trading opportunities since they are deep pullbacks in up-trending markets. Notice that in each case the price pattern of higher highs and higher lows remained intact while the stochastic reached oversold levels. Situations like these warrant close attention because price tends to move sharply higher once the uptrend resumes. Not every situation should be blindly taken when this occurs, however. Always make sure there is an identifiable candlestick pattern to use as a guide to determine good trade entry points as the weight of the evidence methodology increases the odds of making a successful trade.

Relative Strength Index

The *relative strength index* (RSI) was introduced by J. Welles Wilder in 1978. The RSI measures price momentum only and should not be confused with relative strength comparisons from one security or market with another, as is commonly done in inter-market analysis. The RSI is a more robust indicator than the ROC or stochastic because it treats each day in the calculation period as a separate piece in its computation. Recall that the stochastic uses three data points in its computation (the most recent closing price with the high and low for the period), while the ROC only uses two data points (most recent close vs. the close *n* periods ago). The formula for the RSI is $RSI = 100 \times [100/(1+RS)]$, where *RS* is the average of up days divided by the average of down days over the period

Since the RSI uses the *average* of up days versus down days, it is less affected by sharp price moves than the stochastic or ROC. Like the stochastic, the RSI is a banded oscillator with 70 being the default threshold value for an overbought market while the 30 level is the lower band that denotes an oversold market. The longer the period used to compute the RSI, the shallower the momentum swings will be, which means that the overbought and oversold levels will be touched less frequently. For that reason, the upper and lower bands can be adjusted to account for volatility based on the period being examined. For example, when using a 28-day RSI, one may want to adjust the overbought/oversold levels to 65 and 35, respectively. If a five-day RSI is used, the overbought/oversold levels may need to be adjusted to 80/20. Feel free to examine the history of the security or commodity being charted to find threshold values that give the best signals. Range shift is also a consideration for overbought/oversold levels. When using a 14-day RSI in an up-trending market, the overbought/oversold levels are typically 70/40, while in a down-trending market those levels tend to shift downward to 60/30. Again, examine past plots of the RSI to acquaint yourself with these characteristics. Just like the stochastic behavior in uptrends and downtrends, the RSI will show similar patterns.

The concepts of overbought, oversold, and divergence are the same with the RSI as with the stochastic. One of the strengths of the RSI, however, is that it lends itself well to the use of trend lines to track the momentum trend. The daily chart of Cummins Inc. (Fig. 8-12) illustrates this point.

On the left side of the chart, notice that price is performing in a weak manner as it chops lower. The momentum is also falling as shown by the trend line over the top of the RSI. At point A on the price chart, the RSI has managed to break up through its downtrend line, signaling that the downward momentum has shifted and is now moving higher. Also notice that there is a small gravestone doji followed by a rising window that is a bullish candle pattern. The momentum shift along with the candle pattern would be a great

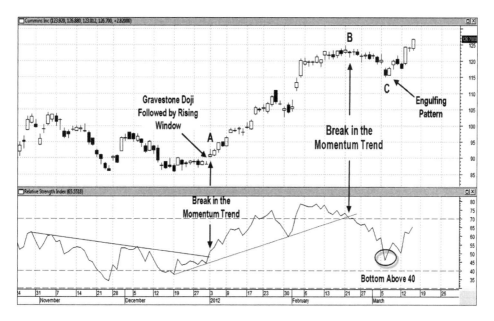

FIGURE 8-12 • RSI Trends: Cummins Inc., Daily
Source: MetaStock

time to initiate a long trade with a protective sell stop just below the low of the gravestone doji.

Price then rose higher into point B. Notice how the RSI trended very nicely between points A and B. When the trend line under the RSI was violated at point B, a signal was given for long traders to consider taking money off the table. Was there a compelling short trade here? Not really, based on the candle patterns or lack thereof. There were a number of doji and spinning tops, but there were no real signals at this point like we had at the low at point A. Another point to make here is that momentum shifts at highs tend to be different events than momentum shifts at lows. Trader psychology in an up-trending market is typically much more sanguine as traders are content and almost serene. This means that tops can take longer to form than bottoms, which are typically more emotional events. Notice the gentle roll of prices after the momentum trend is broken at point B.

After the decline off of point B, price moved lower into the early March low at point C. Following the low at C, price reversed sharply higher. Did you notice where the RSI bottomed at point C? It was well above 40 and closer to 45, an indication of a strong market. An RSI bottom at 40 or higher indicates that upside momentum should be sufficient to carry prices higher. The fact that the RSI bottomed above 40 along with a bullish engulfing pattern provided enough evidence that the uptrend was ready to resume.

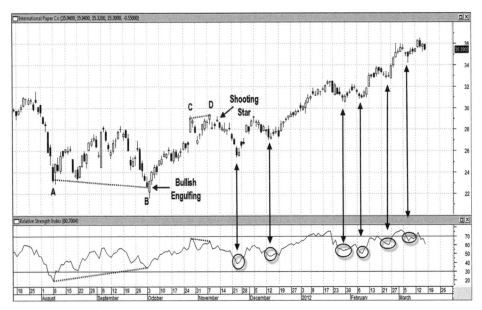

FIGURE 8-13 • RSI Characteristics: International Paper Co., Daily

Source: MetaStock

If we step back and take a look at the longer term implications of the RSI and its patterns, we see that this robust indicator can be a powerful guide for assessing the market landscape. The RSI is a great tool for assessing the strength of momentum for a price trend as well as providing solid clues as to when a change in price direction may be imminent via divergences. The daily chart of International Paper Co. (Fig. 8-13) shows examples of these qualities.

The first area to notice is on the left side of the chart with the line on the price charts marked as A and B. As price made a lower low from point A to point B, the RSI in the lower pane actually made a higher low, which formed a positive momentum divergence with price. The point B was also marked by a bullish engulfing pattern, which showed that trader sentiment was shifting along with price momentum. This created a great buying opportunity and actually marked an important price low September–October 2011.

The line from C to D shows the next divergence—in this case a negative momentum divergence with price. As price pushed out to a new high at point D in November 2011, the RSI made a lower high, which warned that the velocity in price movement was weaker than at the previous high at point C. Also notice the number of small bodied candles that formed as price tried repeatedly to break up through the point C high. This is not the behavior one would like to see in a strong uptrend. As price made its high at point D, there was no compelling signal to initiate a short trade until the shooting star pattern formed three days later. As price broke lower, a short-term top had been made.

As price declined and then reversed higher, however, the RSI showed signs of latent strength. Remember that strength of trend shows itself in the 14-period RSI by the indicator bottoming at 40 or higher. As price declined and then reversed higher, the RSI bottomed at 38.55, which is close enough to 40 considering that International Paper had just emerged from a rather sharp downtrend just a couple of months before. As price continued to advance from there, notice the shallow bottoms that were formed in the RSI as buyers came in to support prices and reinforce the trend.

One note about the momentum indicators shown thus far—always be mindful of the trend when using these indicators as guides. If the trend is up, be very careful with regard to boldly shorting just because a candle reversal pattern appears when a momentum indicator is in overbought territory. When a momentum indicator is in overbought territory in an uptrend, the indicator is merely confirming the strength of the trend. The same can be said with regard to downtrends. If a candle reversal pattern appears in a downtrend with the momentum indicator in oversold territory, be very careful about jumping in with both feet, as the momentum indicator is merely confirming price weakness. When looking to trade against the prevailing trend in the hope of catching a major price reversal, it is best to wait for a candle reversal pattern that forms along with a divergence between price and its momentum. As has been shown, these situations can lead to some very profitable trades.

So far in this chapter, we have covered four of the most used momentum indicators in technical analysis today. Now I would like to present an indicator I developed that has served me well. Before going any further, just be aware that there are people out there who say that indicators are a "dime a dozen" or that "everyone has his or her own little indicators" in an effort to belittle the efforts of anyone who tries to come up with his or her own way of doing things. I have worked with people like that. What these unenlightened individuals fail to realize is that without someone taking the initial step of developing indicators, the four that I have presented in this chapter would not exist. So if these pioneers of technical analysis (Welles Wilder, George Lane, etc.) stepped out and created useful trading tools, why can't we? The bottom line when trying to create homegrown indicators is to have a purpose in mind—in other words, what do you want the indicator to accomplish? What attributes do you want the indicator to have? I encourage you to play with data streams and try to come up with your own ideas, which will then leave you open to your own criticism by others. At that point I will welcome you to the club formed by those of us who think for ourselves. With that said, there is nothing wrong with staying with the classic indicators presented above. What indicators one uses is a personal decision.

Still Struggling?

Choose momentum indicators that fit your trading style.

Choosing the right momentum indicators is a product of understanding your own trading time frame and temperament. For example, if you are a trader who wants to spot and ride longer term trends, the MACD might be a nice choice. If your style is more about spotting shorter term turning points in the market, the ROC or moving average oscillator may be a good fit. The key is understanding the construction and uses of each indicator. There are many to choose from, so take your time and get to know the indicator(s) that pique your interest the most. Understand where they tend to top and bottom in uptrends versus downtrends. See how often they precede or lag price break-outs or breakdowns. Also see how well they interact with their own support or resistance lines. By taking your time and choosing wisely you can have a trusted companion with you when making trading decisions.

High/Low Volatility Indicator

When developing this indicator, I had a list of attributes that I wanted it to have:

1. No boundaries or set scale (i.e., a set scale of 0 to 100)
2. The ability to be directional and trend with price
3. Few whipsaw signals, yet timely enough to catch turning points
4. The ability to see when meaningful changes are occurring in momentum, which leads to changes in the price trend

I did not want a banded oscillator because, while useful, they can be restricted in their movement since the boundaries are set. For example, this means that in a strong uptrend, a stochastic cannot ever go above 100 due to its calculation, but it can "flutter" in the 80s and 90s, which is a sign of strength. In this case, I wanted an indicator that is open ended, just like the price movement it is tracking. This is a cumulative indicator that means that each day's value is added to the existing value of the indicator. This allows it to trend in an open-ended fashion with price.

In addition, I wanted an indicator that has some directionality, or the ability to follow the price trend. Most traders intuitively like to see an indicator track with price or to show a divergence with price movement. In order to accomplish this, some reference to the closing price needs to be included in the formula. There are indicators, for example, that simply measure volatility without regard to price direction. So if price is spiking lower, the indicator could spike to a new high simply because it is measuring raw volatility. If volatility (the variance of price movement) spikes higher regardless of price direction, the indicator will as well. Be aware of that when developing your own indicators.

Attributes 3 and 4 actually go together. Few whipsaw signals should be the goal of anyone who develops an indicator. As always, when filtering out whipsaws by increasing the length of the data stream used in the calculation, some form of lag is introduced. The trade-off is more reliable but slightly less timely signals. I am interested in knowing when momentum is no longer supporting the trend and when price may be ready to turn. Another desired attribute when creating this indicator was to be able to see longer term shifts in market momentum, which can lead to longer term trading opportunities. Candle patterns can be used to help time entry.

The High/Low Volatility I = Yesterday's HLV value + {[(H-L) / 10-Period Moving Average of H–L] × [(C − Previous Close) / Standard Deviation of the last 10 closes]}

What we are doing here is comparing the daily price range (high minus low) to the average of the ranges for the past 10 days. That shows whether or not the most recent range is wider than its average, which shows higher volatility, or narrower than its average, which shows reduced volatility. The comparison of the close from one day to the next against its standard deviation also shows volatility combined with directionality since the first measurement of the closing price shows whether the close was positive or negative versus the prior day. The negative value computed on a down close introduces the ability of the indicator to add a negative number to the series since the high/low value is multiplied by the positive or negative number generated by the comparison of closing prices. By combining the high/low range with its 10-day average, and the price change on a closing basis versus its 10-day standard deviation, large range days with large closing price changes will move the indicator more readily than quiet days with little price movement. These add extra elements to the indicator than others that compare the close to a periodic range (stochastic), or compare the close to previous closing prices (MACD, ROC, and RSI).

If you like this indicator as shown in the examples that follow, plot it on different charts to get to know its characteristics before using it. No indicator is perfect or foolproof. Never just rush out and use an indicator before making sure that it fits your trading style. In the following examples the indicator will be referred to as the HLV indicator.

The daily chart of Citigroup (Fig. 8-14) shows an example of the indicator. Key spots on the chart have been marled with letters A–G. We will begin with a longer term look at the trend and the large degree momentum shift that occurred in November 2011.

FIGURE 8-14 • HLV Indicator: Citigroup Inc., Daily
Source: MetaStock

Point A is the starting point for the section of the downtrend being examined. This acceleration of downward price movement started in May 2011 after a two-month period of sideways price consolidation. Price then declined before rebounding into point B. Skip over point B for now, but we will return to it later. After price rebounded into point C, it then declined, making new lows for the move. Points A and C can then be connected to form the overall downtrend line as well as the corresponding high points at points A and C in the HLV indicator in the bottom pane. Price then rebounded to point D, which was well below the price trend line, but notice that the HLV indicator actually mustered enough strength to rise up and touch its downtrend line. This was a display of latent strength in price momentum that demonstrated the downtrend was beginning to weaken. Price then sold off one more time but failed to make a new low at point E, which was not too surprising since we had already seen signs momentum was beginning to turn.

As price rebounded off of the low at point E, notice that the HLV indicator had broken its six-month trend line, a signal the downtrend in momentum was over. Price then bounced higher before forming a low at point F (the double-sided arrow). The most critical point to make here is that the HLV indicator showed that what was once resistance (the downtrend line) was now support as momentum bounced higher from there. A longer term trade could have been entered there with a protective sell stop below the low at point E since momentum had turned and was now positive. Had a trader waited solely for price to break its downtrend line, that would not have occurred until two months later at point G.

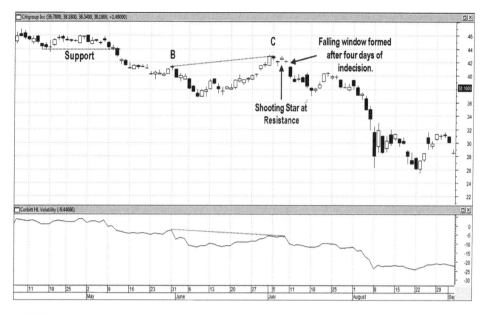

FIGURE 8-15 • HLV Indicator Trade: Citigroup Inc., Daily
Source: MetaStock

Now that we have stepped back and taken a longer term look at the indicator, let's zero in on a great shorter term trading opportunity that presented itself between points B and C. Figure 8-15 zooms in on the B to C section of the chart shown in Fig. 8-14. Notice that price had already begun its downtrend as price took out its prior support level of 44 on the upper left portion of the chart. Price rebounded into point B before declining one more time and then rebounding into the point C high. If one was looking purely at price, was this a sign that a low may have been posted since the high at point C was higher than at point B? The HLV indicator said no. Notice how it made a lower high at its corresponding point while price made a higher high. This is where we can use our candlestick analysis to help time a trade entry. After the high at point C, notice how price chopped sideways for four days, forming two hanging men, a shooting star at resistance, and a doji. These were hardly compelling signals that the bulls were ready to push Citigroup higher at that point. Following the period of obvious indecision, price then gapped lower forming a falling window, which meant that the downtrend was ready to resume. A short trade could have been entered either off of the shooting star pattern, or following the falling window with a protective buy stop placed above the high at point B.

It is important to note that none of the momentum indicators covered previously would have shown this divergence. This includes the RSI, ROC, stochastic oscillator, or MACD. This is not a knock against these other classic mainstream indicators, merely a statement that sometimes thinking outside the box can serve you well.

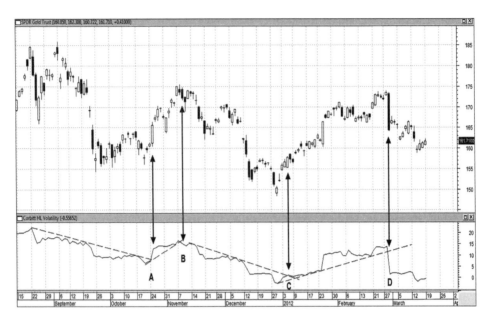

FIGURE 8-16 • HLV Indicator Trades: SPDR Gold Trust ETF, Daily
Source: MetaStock

As you have seen by now, the HLV indicator lends itself well to the use of trend lines. When these lines are broken, that marks a shift in the price momentum trend, which typically leads to a change in price direction. This quality is not just for use in longer term scenarios, it can also be used in shorter term time frames to show short-term shifts in momentum that can be exploited for profit when paired with candle patterns. The daily chart of the SPDR Gold Trust ETF (Fig. 8-16) shows an example of how the HLV indicator can be used to gain a clearer look at the momentum that is driving the price action, which can help confirm shifts in price direction. These trend line breaks and candle patterns typically coincide with each other, creating a weight of the evidence situation that leads to better quality trades than trading on candle patterns or indicator readings alone.

Prior to point A, price had been behaving in a choppy, erratic fashion as shown on the left side of the chart. If you take a look at the HLV indicator, however, you will see that it is in a very recognizable, smooth-looking downtrend as it made a series of lower highs and lower lows. By connecting the tops of the bounces in the HLV indicator, an effective downtrend line could be drawn to alert a trader when price momentum was in the process of shifting. As price came into the low just prior to point A, a doji formed that could have been classified as a morning star or abandoned baby, but the real body was too long. So instead of possibly labeling the pattern incorrectly, let's just say it was a doji reversal.

As price reversed, two small bodied candles formed, each after a rising window. While a trade could have been placed following the formation of the doji reversal pattern with a protective sell stop below the doji just to the left of point A, a more conservative trader could have waited for the momentum trend to change as well. This is what happened three days after the doji as a long white candle formed. This was the first time in over a month that buyers had dominated the action like that, and the shift in the momentum trend verified it as the HLV indicator broke its downtrend line.

Price then advanced higher until the uptrend line on the HLV indicator was broken at point B. Just prior to point B, a long white candle formed followed by a bearish harami. The very next day a long black candle formed, signifying that sellers were stepping up to apply downside pressure. The formation of the long black candle at point B also caused the HLV indicator to break its uptrend line. An interesting note here is that this trend line break at point B could have simply been used to lock in trading profits if the trader desired. More aggressive traders would now look to play the short side while also placing a protective buy stop just above the high of the long white candle just prior to point B.

Following the break of the rising trend line at point B, price then declined again until the momentum trend shifted at point C. Just to the left of point C, a white candle formed the low as price gapped lower; it then reversed and gapped higher the next day, forming what is known as an island reversal in Western technical analysis. Again, at the breaking of the downtrend line on the HLV indicator at point C, a short trader could have simply booked profits while a more aggressive trader could have followed with a new long trade. As the HLV indicator broke higher, notice the corresponding candle pattern that closely resembled a three white soldiers pattern. This is a powerful reversal signal that shows strong buying support. If a trader had not initiated a long position following the island reversal, this would now be the time as evidence of strong buying pressure and a shift in the momentum trend combined to show that market sentiment had indeed changed for the near term. A protective sell stop should have been placed below the low of the island reversal pattern. Price then advanced into point D where a huge black candle showed that sellers had rushed for the exits. Still, any positions initiated following the three white soldiers at point C could have been closed for a small profit.

Adding the HLV indicator to your trading arsenal can provide you with an extra edge into price momentum that may not be evident by using some of the more traditional indicators we covered earlier in the chapter. Whether you see value in using this indicator is up to you. I merely wanted to present another way of using momentum indicators. It trends well and does not react as sharply as some of the other momentum indicators to wild swings in prices. The beauty of trading is that you can set up your own indicators that fit your trading style, temperament, and time frame. Just remember to always get to know the behavior tendencies of the indicators you use before trusting them on the field of battle in the markets.

Since this is a book on candlestick charting, I have only presented some commonly used momentum indicators (and a new one) with the intention of complementing candlestick patterns and signals. An entire book could be devoted to this topic, and in fact many have been written. My all time favorite is *Martin Pring on Market Momentum* by Martin J. Pring. I strongly suggest this book for anyone who wants a deep-rooted understanding of momentum indicators and their many uses. Momentum indicators can provide invaluable insight for traders, but they are not foolproof. For that reason it is always best to pair their signals with candle patterns and to always use protective stops when trading.

Summary

- Momentum indicators measure the rate or velocity at which prices move up or down.
- Momentum indicators are not foolproof, which is why stops should be used on every trade.
- Their uses include displaying overbought/oversold levels, revealing divergences, and analyzing the overall momentum trend.
- Oscillators come in two types: banded and centered.
- The MACD is a centered momentum oscillator that consists of the difference between two moving averages.
- The rate of change is a centered oscillator that compares the current closing price to the closing price *n* periods ago.
- The stochastic is a banded oscillator that measures the closing price against its price range for the period.
- The RSI is a banded oscillator that uses the average of up days versus down days over the period being computed.
- The HLV is an indicator that trends well with price and can help traders spot turning points in the market.
- Select the momentum indicator that best fits your trading style, temperament, and time frame.

QUIZ

1. Which momentum indicator is also classified as a centered oscillator?
   A. Stochastic
   B. RSI
   C. Rate of change
   D. None of the above

2. It is advisable to enter trades purely on signals from momentum indicators.
   A. True
   B. False

3. The MACD is a fast-moving indicator.
   A. True
   B. False

4. Which indicator compares today's closing price to the closing price n days ago?
   A. Rate of change
   B. RSI
   C. MACD
   D. Stochastic

5. Which momentum indicator is the difference between two moving averages?
   A. HLV
   B. Stochastic
   C. RSI
   D. MACD

6. Which momentum indicator shows divergences with price?
   A. Stochastic
   B. HLV
   C. RSI
   D. All of the above

7. Which momentum indicator measures the closing price against the high/low range for the period?
   A. RSI
   B. Rate of change
   C. Stochastic
   D. MACD

8. Whipsaw signals are a concern that one needs to be aware of when using momentum indicators.
   A. True
   B. False

9. **Momentum indicators should not be included in the weight of the evidence trading concept.**
   A. True
   B. False

10. **If a momentum indicator shows a divergence with price, which statement is true?**
    A. It is a guaranteed reversal trade—take it.
    B. It is merely an indication that price momentum is slowing.
    C. It should be ignored.
    D. None of the above

Chapter 9

Candlesticks and Volume

Just as the eyes are the window into the soul, volume is the window into trader sentiment. Volume is a very important, yet often overlooked, component of market analysis. With the large number of price momentum indicators, some of which were covered in Chapter 8, volume analysis is often relegated to the back burner when it comes to understanding trader behavior. With that said, volume data have also lost some of their integrity over the past few years due to the proliferation of high-frequency trading, but volume can still be an effective tool when analyzed *over time*.

CHAPTER OBJECTIVES

In this chapter, you will

- Understand volume analysis and its value in understanding market psychology
- Learn methods of volume analysis
- Use and understand volume based indicators
- Combine volume analysis with candle patterns for more effective trading

Since we have already established that candlestick charting provides a deeper look into the mindset of traders, combining what we already know with volume analysis should provide even more information to use to make sound trading decisions. In this chapter you will learn the importance of volume, its characteristics, and other indicators that include volume in their calculation, including another "homegrown" indicator I find quite valuable.

While candle patterns show the mindset of traders at key reversal or continuation points in the market, volume provides the backdrop, or the mood of the market, as price moves progress. In trending markets, volume is a valuable piece of the analysis puzzle. In a rather overused but accurate analogy, think of volume to a trend in the same way one thinks of gasoline to a car. With no fuel, the car would not run. If, during the journey, one notices that the gas supply is getting low, a valid assumption can be made that the journey will not continue much farther unless more gas is added to the tank. In much the same way, buyers are needed to push price higher, while sellers are needed to push price lower. If volume is decreasing as a trend progresses, that is a sign that the tank is getting low and that more fuel needs to be added (in the form of more buyers or sellers emerging) for the trend to continue.

Remember that volume is best used as a tool over time to assess the strength of market trends. That means that volume patterns should be studied for clues as to whether change may be on the way. For example, if volume is steadily increasing throughout an uptrend but then begins to decrease as price continues to move higher, that is a sign that the fuel necessary to continue to push price higher may be decreasing as less buyers are present to support the trend. Also, if volume is steady throughout an uptrend, an increase or decrease in volume needs to be watched closely. Why? That is because volume characteristics have changed. One of the most common misconceptions about volume is that during uptrends, volume needs to be constantly expanding for uptrends to continue. On the contrary, it is perfectly acceptable for volume to remain steady as price advances. It is when the volume *pattern* changes that traders need to pay close attention.

With regard to downtrends, another misconception is that volume needs to expand during downtrends for price to continue to fall. In downtrends, price can fall under its own weight due simply to a lack of buying interest. In fact when volume expands as downtrends mature, that is typically evidence of some form of panic, which means that a bottom may be near as everyone who planned on selling has sold their positions as the downside momentum reaches a crescendo.

Volume Patterns

Volume measures the conviction that traders have as they collectively move the market. Volume combined with price shows the activity of the herd and how strongly they feel about price movement. Increasing volume totals can "validate" certain price movements such as breakouts or reversals. Volume also

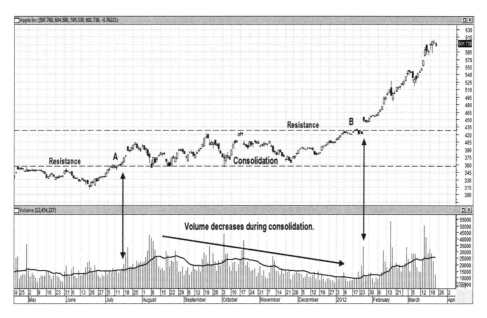

FIGURE 9-1 • Volume Patterns: Apple Inc., Daily
Source: MetaStock

tends to dry up during periods of consolidation or indecision. The daily chart of Apple Inc. (Fig. 9-1) shows an example of different volume patterns as price moves develop.

One of the tools used to analyze volume patterns is the volume moving average (VMA). As volume increases or decreases over time, the VMA reflects those changes. This is the same moving average concept applied to price data in Chapter 7, but now it is being applied to volume data. Figure 9-1 shows a 20-day VMA overlaid on the volume plot in the lower pane.

On the price chart there are two horizontal dashed lines that represent resistance levels price needed to overcome if it was going to continue to move higher. Notice at point A as price broke through the bottom horizontal resistance line that volume increased sharply as shown by the spike in the individual volume bars. That volume spike provided validation that there were enough buyers to absorb the supply of shares for sale just under the 360 level. Price then moved sideways for more than six months before breaking out above the second resistance line at point B. Once again notice the spike in volume as buyers provided the necessary fuel for price to overcome resistance near the 430 level.

Throughout the chart as this pattern unfolded, notice the behavior of the 20-day VMA. As price was preparing for a breakthrough resistance at point A, the VMA was rather flat with a slight upward bias. As price consolidated between points A and B, volume contracted markedly as buyers and sellers exchanged shares during a period of rest for the price move. The low volume marked this period as one of indecision as neither buyers nor sellers had the necessary conviction to move price in either direction. Finally, notice the movement in the VMA after the breakout at point B. As price exploded over resistance, volume expanded with price, which was demonstrated by the steady ascent of the VMA as price moved higher. This was a sign of increasing buyer interest, which pushed Apple shares sharply higher over the next two months.

Still Struggling

Volume cannot always be trusted.

When a stock or exchange-traded fund (ETF) is thinly traded (this is known as *low liquidity* or *illiquid*), the price of that stock or ETF is open to manipulation. The general rule that I use is that if the 20-day VMA is less than 200,000 shares per day, then volume analysis becomes suspect. Another thing to look for when analyzing charts is repeated days of erratic volume behavior with little or no price movement. If you can't detect a volume pattern over time, be very careful when trading. Thinly traded (illiquid) stocks can also make it very difficult to get a fair price when buying or selling. Some futures contracts, on the other hand, have lower daily volume totals, which would preclude them from the minimum 200,000 daily volume limit, such as pork bellies. The key is to look for a consistent volume pattern. The bottom line is to know what you trade and trade what you know.

Let's take one more look at how the change in volume patterns can help a trader identify periods of change in the market. The daily chart of Flowserve Corp. (Fig. 9-2) contains some examples. Notice first on the left side of the chart how price was in a steady downtrend May–June 2011. The double-sided arrow points to the corresponding volume area at the bottom of the chart. What do you notice? This was a strong trend, but it did not need increasing volume as price fell during the trend. Price was falling under its own weight as buyers were not willing to step up to support prices. This meant that traders were in agreement that Flowserve needed to reach lower levels to attract enough new buyers to stabilize price.

As price continued lower, volume began to increase as price approached what turned out to be the point A low. Increasing volume as price initially reversed lower would normally be a bearish event, but in this case, the volume pattern had already been established during the downtrend, which was a steady, consistent volume pace as price declined. The increase in volume was a change in the way price and volume were interacting—a signal that something had

FIGURE 9-2 • Volume Patterns: Flowserve Inc., Daily

Source: MetaStock

changed in trader perception of Flowserve as price approached the $80 level. The increase in volume could be either increased short covering as shorts lock in profits or an increase in new buying activity because better value was seen at these levels. Whatever the reason, volume spiked higher over a two-week period as the low at point A formed. Would this be the final low before price reversed and moved higher? There was no way to tell yet.

Following the low at point A, price consolidated in a sideways movement through the end of July, which is marked by point B on the chart. Notice that volume settled down as price chopped sideways, signaling a period of consolidation. As price broke lower out of the range by violating the support line drawn off of the point A low, volume increased once again, this time spiking even higher as price formed another low at point C. The low at point C showed even more activity than the low at point A, as demonstrated by the increase in volume.

Following the low at point C, price rebounded again to form another consolidation range as volume receded to lower levels. Following the brief consolidation, price broke lower one more time into the low at point D. Something very important happened at point D, however. Notice that volume peaked at a much lower level than it had at point C as shown by the dotted line in the volume pane. That was a sure sign that selling pressure had diminished and the downtrend was nearing an end. You will see that following the low at point D, volume dropped off markedly before increasing again, this time as price pushed *higher*. This showed that the tide had turned and that buyers were entering the market expecting higher prices.

Following the low at point D, price then began a five-month uptrend. Notice the volume pattern in the lower pane. Once again, expanding volume was not needed for the uptrend to continue. It was simply a steady pattern that became one of the characteristics of the uptrend. It was when volume spiked higher at point E in March 2012 that traders were made aware of a change in trader behavior. The normal, steady pattern that was in place since November 2011 had changed. This meant that traders needed to be on the lookout for a possible change in price direction as sellers were likely stepping up their activity. Sure enough, change was apparent as price violated its uptrend line and began to move lower.

This example is not to show that volume should be steady in every uptrend or downtrend. The purpose here is to show that each uptrend or downtrend has its own volume pattern. A trader needs to get a feel for what that pattern is in each individual case. Is volume expanding as price rises or falls, or is volume steady as price rises or falls? In either case, it is when that pattern *changes* that a trader can be tipped off to changes in trader sentiment. Now that we have looked at broad examples of volume, let's take a look at some indicators that include volume in their calculations and see how they can be used with candlestick patterns.

Still Struggling

Volume analysis is valuable, but there are times when it does not give the complete picture.

While volume is a very valuable tool to look into the mindset of traders, there are times when it does not give the full picture. For example, if price reverses higher off of a deep low on high volume, it is virtually impossible to tell if such action was due to short covering or new traders taking up positions because of good valuation. The odds typically favor the former in a volatile reversal as short covering (those that were forced to buy back shares that they previously sold short) provides fuel in sharp reversals, but again, there is no way to know for sure. Also, the practice of high-frequency trading tends to inflate volume totals and can skew otherwise sound analysis. Periods of low volume, however, are more certain. Periods of low volume can mean only one thing—that trader interest is low, which makes strong price moves on low volume suspect. On the other hand, low volume periods with rather dull price movement can alert a trader that a sharp move in one direction or the other may be on the way. Remember to use a VMA to get a feel for what the average volume amount is over the time period you are analyzing. Values below the VMA can be categorized as lighter volume, while values above the VMA can be categorized as heavier volume.

Money Flow Index

The money flow index (MFI) is a banded oscillator that combines price and volume data to measure buying and selling pressure. Created by Gene Quong and Avrum Soudack, the MFI is essentially a volume-weighted relative strength index (RSI). Just about any competent charting software application can plot an MFI indicator with just a couple of mouse clicks. The typical default values for the MFI are 80 for the overbought zone and 20 for oversold.

The daily chart of Flowserve used in the previous example has been expanded in Fig. 9-3 to provide a larger scope of data to show just how the MFI works. There are two main points of interest marked A and B. Let's start at the very left of the chart, prior to point A. Price was in a strong uptrend as shown by higher highs and higher lows. Take a look at the 14-day MFI in the middle pane. Remember how we said in Chapter 8 that momentum indicators tend to reflect the trend by where they top or bottom? During the uptrend, the MFI tended to bottom between 40 and 50, while topping around the 80 level as marked by the upper thin solid line on the MFI plot. Point A at the top of the chart was where a major top had formed in Flowserve in March 2011. Notice how the MFI had already begun moving sharply lower as price headed into resistance at its prior high. The MFI was indicating that the upward momentum necessary to continue the rally had completely dissipated and was now heading south. That was an indication that the market was ready for a rather sharp turn. We will focus on that opportunity and the candlestick patterns that went with it in the next chart example.

Staying with Fig. 9-3, take a look at the low at point B. That was the low we examined in Fig. 9-2 in which volume was not as strong as it was at the previous low, showing that trader psychology had changed. The MFI picked up the difference as it flashed a positive divergence as price made a lower low but the indicator did not. This is where the volume component served us well as it showed that the volume push was not as strong at the point B low, which preceded a major turn.

Finally, notice how the range in the MFI shifted as price went from uptrend to downtrend and back to uptrend. This shows the tendency of the MFI to reflect the trend as it bottomed in the 40–50 range during uptrends and topped in the 60–70 range during downtrends. It is when these boundaries are violated that one can expect a change in price direction.

Now let's take a closer look at the April 2011 high in Flowserve that was at point A in the previous chart. Figure 9-4 shows that price made its initial high in early April, followed by a shallow sell off and one more push up into resistance. There were a few things to note here in using our weight of the evidence methodology. First, as price pushed higher into the resistance area formed by the prior high, three straight small bodied candles formed—two doji and one spinning top. As price encountered the previous high, shown by the horizontal dotted line, a

FIGURE 9-3 • MFI: Flowserve Inc., Daily

Source: MetaStock

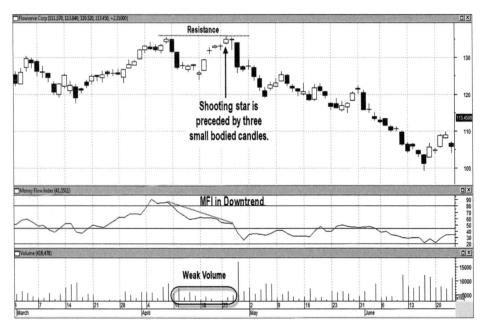

FIGURE 9-4 • MFI Trade: Flowserve Inc., Daily

Source: MetaStock

shooting star formed. At the same time, look at the 14-day MFI in the middle pane. As price moved higher, the MFI deteriorated sharply and was heading decisively lower. A solid horizontal line has been added at the 45 level in the MFI plot to demonstrate when the characteristics of the MFI changed following the reversal. Notice prior to the formation of the high, the MFI was bottoming in the 40–45 area. After price reversed and began moving lower, the MFI began *topping* in the same area, demonstrating a very weak market.

Typically in bear markets, the MFI will top out at a higher level than that (60–70 as stated above), but this behavior showed the intense selling pressure being applied to Flowserve shares at the time. Finally, notice how light volume was on the push into resistance (circled below). The light volume showed almost nonexistent conviction among buyers. So here is what we have with our weight of the evidence methodology:

1. Price was pushing higher into resistance while forming two doji, a spinning top, and a shooting star.
2. The MFI had already reversed and was heading lower, which showed a tremendous deterioration of upside momentum.
3. Volume was very light, showing almost no conviction among buyers as price encountered resistance.

A short trade could have been entered after price moved below the real body of the shooting star candle with a protective buy stop placed over the high of the shooting star candle. For less aggressive traders, this would have been a great signal to exit long positions.

Accumulation/Distribution Line

The accumulation/distribution line (AD line) was developed by Marc Chaikin and quantifies whether shares or futures contracts are being accumulated (bought) or distributed (sold) by traders. This cumulative indicator has a price momentum component that is amplified by volume activity. The AD line is good for confirming overall trend and looking for turning points. While this is not the best tool to use with the shorter term signals generated by candlestick patterns, some great trades can still be made, and this indicator is also the foundation for two other indicators developed by Chaikin that are much more effective when paired with candlesticks. The AD line also has a center or zero line, but one is not advised to use crossovers for trading signals due to the cumulative nature of the indicator. Also, the proximity of the zero line to current values can vary depending on the starting point for plotting AD line values.

Computing the AD line is a two-step process. First, one must compute the close location value (CLV):

$$CLV = [(close - low) - (high - close)] / (high - low)$$

The CLV has a possible range of values from −1 to 1. The value of 1 is attained when price closes at its high for the period, while the value of −1 reflects when price closed at its low for the period. The second step of the computation results in the AD line value and is calculated as follows:

AD line = yesterday's AD line value + (CLV × volume for the period)

The daily chart of Honeywell International Inc. (Fig. 9-5) shows an example of the AD line and how it reflects the trend, but the chart also shows how the AD line can show divergences that can lead to very profitable trading opportunities. First notice on the very left side of the chart how price was moving lower off of its late April 2010 high, but the AD line was moving higher. This showed latent accumulation of shares by traders as the price declined, which set the stage for the powerful uptrend that followed. As price moved higher, the AD line began showing negative divergences from February to April 2011. Following the initial February peak, price then pushed higher, forming two higher peaks, but the AD line had already turned and begun a slow descent. The negative divergence warned that even though price was pushing higher, traders were actually unloading shares. This backdrop preceded the fierce downtrend that followed.

Figure 9-6 zeroes in on the April 2011 top in Honeywell Inc. to show how divergences in the AD line can lead to great profit opportunities. Whenever attempting to trade using candlesticks and the AD line, always remember that an element of patience is required. The AD line is a longer term indicator, and

FIGURE 9-5 • AD Line: Honeywell Inc., Daily
Source: MetaStock

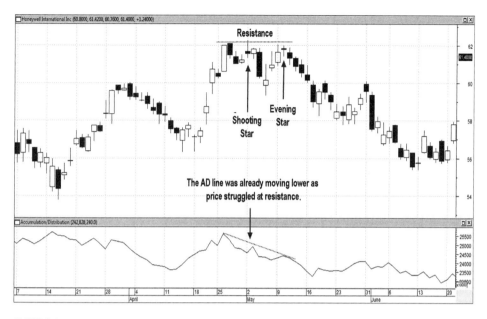

FIGURE 9-6 • AD Trade: Honeywell Inc., Daily

Source: MetaStock

the short-term nature of candlesticks can sometimes not synch up well with AD line movements, which can result in losing trades. This is why stops should always be used. But do not be afraid to trade the next candle reversal pattern as long as the AD line continues to show the same characteristics as the last trade. The AD line is a reliable indicator at turning points; however, it sometimes takes a little bit of time for price to reflect the change in trader activity as shown by the indicator.

Notice first as price advanced into its late April high at the very top of the chart that it reversed lower on what could be classified as a thrusting pattern. That by itself did not signal a price reversal, but it did set a short-term resistance line as price consolidated for two days before making another run at that level. On the third day following the thrusting line, price made another move higher, but this time formed a shooting star as price temporarily broke over the previous high but closed poorly as sellers unloaded shares. One could place a trade two days later on the formation of the long black candle with a protective stop just above the high of the shooting star. Since at the time there is a "hard right edge" on the chart the day the trade was made, a trader has no idea what to expect next, which is why the stop orders serve so well in controlling risk. Remember that each example shown is neat and tidy in hindsight, but in real-time trading, one does not know what the market will serve up next.

Following the long black candle, price then rallied for three days, which would have been discouraging for a trader with a brand-new short position. The third day, however, an evening star pattern formed once again at prior resistance. The confirmation of the reversal the next day started a waterfall decline that saw Honeywell lose more than 9 percent of its value over the next month.

Using the AD line can give a trader clues as to whether or not the action of traders is leading to a change in price direction. The AD line is not the best indicator to use with candlesticks due to its long-term nature, but it is the basis for the next two indicators we will examine, the Chaikin AD oscillator and Chaikin money flow.

Chaikin AD Oscillator

The Chaikin AD oscillator (ADO) is a derivative of the AD line and is used to show turning points in the market in short to intermediate time frames. The ADO is computed by subtracting a 10-period exponential moving average of the AD line from a 3-period exponential moving average of the AD line. This result in a centered oscillator where crossovers of the zero line result in buy and sell signals.

Let's examine the ADO by plotting the indicator on the same chart used in Fig. 9-6. Figure 9-7 shows the same price chart of Honeywell Inc., only this time the ADO has been added in the middle pane. The first thing you may notice is that the ADO tends to trace out the same pattern as the longer term AD line, but the ADO is plotted on a much more compact scale with the presence of a zero line to give a trader much better perspective on short-term market behavior.

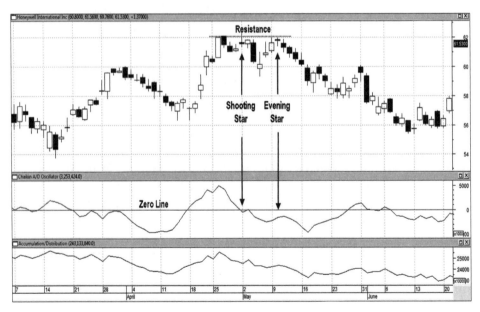

FIGURE 9-7 • ADO Trade: Honeywell Inc., Daily

Source: MetaStock

Notice at the formation of the shooting star that the ADO had crossed the zero line and was already in "sell" territory (below the zero line) as the shooting star formed. Following the shooting star pattern, the ADO moved even lower as price tried a second time to overcome resistance, which resulted in the formation of the evening star pattern. In this case, the ADO did a tremendous job of quantifying the weakness that was shown by two consecutive candle reversal patterns that formed at resistance.

By itself, an indicator showing a divergence is not reason enough to jump into a trade, however. Remember that no indicator is foolproof, and unnecessary losses can result if a trader gets an itchy trigger finger. Again, this is an after the fact example, but try to visualize each phase of this analysis, even if it means covering up the chart to the right of whatever section we are discussing, just to give you that element of uncertainty as to what will happen next in real-time trading.

The daily chart of KB Home in Fig. 9-8 shows an example of the ADO giving the indication that a bottom was very near as it flashed a positive divergence with price. That is one piece of evidence, but take a look at the price plot at the time of the divergence. What candle pattern do you see there to alert a trader that a change in direction may be coming? If you answered none, you would be correct. Just because a divergence occurs, that is no reason to get excited and jump into a trade. Recall in previous examples that numerous divergences can form before price changes direction. Also, even if price does get a short-term pop following a divergence, there is no guarantee as to how high price will go.

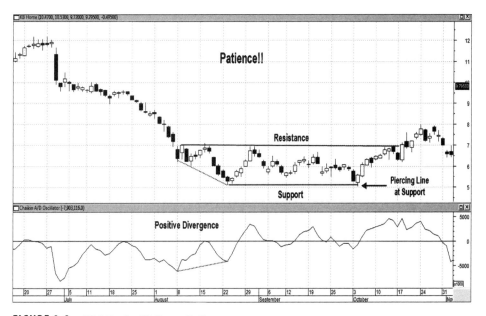

FIGURE 9-8 • ADO Trade: KB Home Daily

Source: MetaStock

Following the divergence, price moved sideways as it established a range of support and resistance. A disciplined trader would still be watching the price movement to look for clues as to which way price would break out of the range.

One other thing to notice as price chopped sideways between support and resistance is the range shift that took place in the ADO. On the left side of the chart, the range was much lower as the ADO topped at or near the zero line, showing latent weakness. As price chopped sideways, however, the ADO began *bottoming* near the zero area—a sign of strength.

As price came down to the bottom of the range in early October, a bullish piercing line formed. This was our first real buy signal since the divergence formed between ADO and price back in August. Yes, there was resistance looming overhead, but we had a solid buy signal with a lower risk entry as the protective sell stop could have been placed just below the low of the piercing line. Price then managed to grind higher before breaking through resistance two weeks later, which resulted in price appreciation of 45 percent from the low of the piercing line to the high three weeks later.

Chaikin Money Flow

Chaikin money flow (CMF) is also a centered oscillator that is derived from the calculated values of the AD line and is typically computed over a 21-day period. The CMF is simply the summation of the last 21 days of the AD line divided by the sum of the last 21 days of volume. You can, however, compute the CMF over any time period you wish to suit your purposes. We will use the common default period of 21 days in the following examples. Values above the zero line show periods of market strength while values below the zero line show periods of market weakness.

The daily chart of Raytheon Co. (Fig. 9-9) shows an example of the CMF. This is a similar setup in the same time frame in which we examined the ADO with Honeywell in Fig. 9-8. First, once again notice the range shift from the left side of the chart (uptrend—CMF primarily above zero) to the right side of the chart (downtrend—CMF primarily below zero). As price transitioned from uptrend to downtrend from January to March 2011, the CMF weakened considerably as price twice tried to break through resistance. On the first try to break through resistance, a beautiful evening star formed, and on the second try, a shooting star formed. As each pattern formed, the CMF remained below zero. That is a significant momentum event with price attempting to break out to new highs.

Now let's zoom in on the reversal area in Fig. 9-9 where Raytheon formed its top and examine the two reversal patterns there. First, as price approached the resistance set in January 2011 on the left side of the chart, the evening star pattern formed as the CMF broke below zero. That was a compelling looking evening star, and, quite frankly, I would have traded it with a protective buy

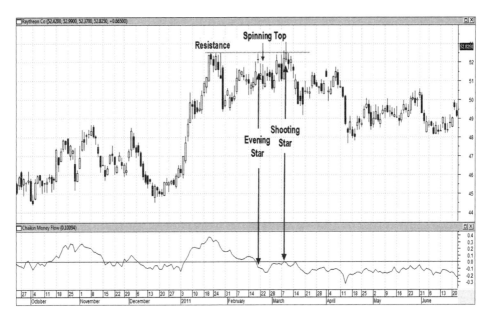

FIGURE 9-9 • CMF: Raytheon Co., Daily
Source: MetaStock

stop just above the evening star high. The first sign that this reversal may take a while or not work at all came the day following the completion of the evening star pattern when a spinning top formed. This showed wide-swinging emotions with little downside movement when all was said and done for the day. Price then chopped sideways for nine more days before breaking through resistance on an intra-day basis. That may have been all that was needed to have the stop price triggered and cause one to settle for a small loss. The very next day a shooting star formed with a long upper shadow. Price once again failed to close above resistance, however, while the CMF remained below the zero line. The following day, price gapped lower, forming a falling window, but price once again formed a spinning top, hardly compelling evidence to put on another short trade. However, the other things to consider were that the CMF was still below the zero line, price had failed to close above resistance, and this was a relatively low-risk opportunity to take another shot, since the protective buy stop would have been placed just above the high of the shooting star.

Remember what I said earlier about not being afraid to try again if a trade gets stopped out and a similar opportunity presents itself? We essentially have the same setup as the first trade. If one had taken the second trade, it would have been profitable even though it took nearly a month for price to break considerably lower. This example is a great one to show the short-term difficulties that can develop when price does not behave as we would like it to. There is nothing to be gained by showing you a series of home run trades that act exactly as we want them to. In fact, even if one had taken the second trade,

FIGURE 9-10 • CMF Trades: Raytheon Co., Daily
Source: MetaStock

the incessant chop in prices may have been enough to cause the trader to close out the trade and go look for a better opportunity elsewhere. That is a reason for making sure you define and stick to your time horizon for trading. For example, if you are comfortable holding a position for only a few days, you would have exited before the larger break lower occurred. If your time horizon was that of a longer term position trader, you may have held the position for six weeks or more.

Volume Percent Positive

Volume percent positive (VPP) is an indicator I developed to quantify volume with price movement. It is a simple indicator to compute and understand, yet it can reveal changes in volume patterns at key times in the market. Its primary purpose is to determine if volume patterns are in synch with price movements, or if changing volume patterns indicate that a change in price direction may be near. I wanted a banded oscillator type of indicator on a standardized scale to show when volume totals were reaching extreme levels and a shift in volume patterns may emerge. I also wanted an indicator that would not be easily distorted by high volume spikes that can sometimes alter volume plots and indicators to the point of being useless for trend analysis due to tremendous changes in indicator values. This indicator adjusts to either high or low volume periods by simply plotting the percentage of total volume, which keeps everything relative to whatever environment the stock or futures contract is in. The VPP is an indicator that can be computed using the volume of a single stock or futures contract.

The computation of VPP treats volume as all positive for the day if a day's closing price is higher than the previous day, or all negative if a day's closing price is lower than the previous day. The indicator can be computed over a 10-day period, a 20-day period, or whatever time period one desires. The formula is

Sum of positive volume over n periods / sum of total volume over n periods

The result can be a plotted line that is sometimes jagged and volatile at turning points, so I like to smooth the indicator with a three-day simple moving average, using the 70 level and above as overbought and the 30 level and below as oversold. The daily chart of the SPDR Gold Trust ETF (Fig. 9-11) shows a plot of the VPP in the lower pane. There are some points on the chart that are noteworthy. First notice that the huge momentum high in September 2011 was not confirmed by positive volume. The VPP actually peaked a month before in early August. Then it began moving lower even as price exploded into its September high. This indicator should be treated as any other. Just because it flashes a divergence with price does not mean that a trade should be blindly entered. It does, however, provide a warning to those insisting on staying long that the risk of loss is moving higher with price as volume fails to confirm the price move.

FIGURE 9-11 • VPP Indicator: SPDR Gold Trust ETF, Daily

Source: MetaStock

The second highlight is evident at the times when the VPP reached the oversold level (below 30) just before price and volume both turned higher into the next rally phase. Again, just because the VPP reaches oversold levels is no reason to get excited and get long. It is, however, an indication that if other pieces of a weight of the evidence methodology say that it is time to put on a trade, it can be done with a higher degree of confidence.

The next example is a daily chart of Verizon Communications (Fig. 9-12) that shows how the VPP indicator can be used with support and resistance lines to determine whether volume flows are continuing or reversing. On the chart you will see that the 20-day VPP has dotted support and resistance lines drawn over tops and bottoms to get a feel for the short-term volume trend. Notice how each time one of the lines is violated, price changes direction, except for the violation of the support line at point X (marked in the VPP window). At point X there were no candle reversal signals, plus price had been declining for eight days before the VPP broke its support line, so it was not the most opportune time to place a trade. We are interested in finding opportunities that show that a reversal is likely based on the weight of the evidence. Following point X, volume quickly turned positive again, which carried price to its late December high.

At each double-sided arrow, the volume pattern changed direction, but in some cases, the VPP served to confirm a price reversal that had already occurred (point A), or it turned concurrently with price. Even when the VPP turns concurrently with price, it provides a powerful confirmation that the

FIGURE 9-12 • VPP Indicator Support and Resistance: Verizon Communications, Daily
Source: MetaStock

fuel necessary to drive trends (volume) is changing course and can allow one to trade candle reversal patterns with more confidence. When the tide of volume begins to change, price is almost certain to react. There are also three points on the chart marked A, B, and C. We will zero in on those areas to look for trading opportunities by combining the VPP with candle reversal patterns.

Figure 9-13 zeroes in on points A, B, and C from Fig. 9-12. Point X is marked as well on the far right of the chart merely to serve as a point of reference to gain perspective as to where we are on the chart. You will also notice the support and resistance lines have been placed in the same spot, with the exception of a shorter term support line up to point B that was not present on the previous chart. The point here is that with the VPP, wherever you can get a support or resistance line in by connecting two highs or lows, draw it in. I purposely did not do that in Fig. 9-12 so as to not add confusion to the longer term chart.

Beginning at the left side of the chart prior to point A, notice that there is a break of the support line in VPP following the first high to the left of point A. At that first high, there was no real candle pattern to trade off of, just a series of sloppy candles as price chopped lower. That was no time to place a trade even though VPP had turned lower with price. Just because VPP turns lower does not mean that an all-out reversal is coming. It could simply mean that traders are taking a rest before resuming the uptrend. Since there was no candle pattern of note, it was best to stand aside and let the situation sort itself out.

FIGURE 9-13 • VPP Indicator Trades: Verizon Communications Daily

Source: MetaStock

After a brief pullback, price then moved sharply higher into point A. With the high to the left of point A now forming resistance, the evening star pattern that formed had even more meaning. A candle formation like that is compelling on its own, but look at what was happening on the VPP. As price moved higher with three straight smaller bodied candles into resistance, *the VPP was still moving lower*—an indication that volume flows were not supporting the rally. That was a great shorting opportunity with a protective buy stop placed above the high of the evening star candle.

Next let's take a look at point B. This was a situation where drawing a shorter term support line can help with a trade entry. Notice first that the longer term support line drawn off of the August low in the VPP was not in danger of being violated, so the longer term movement in volume flows was still higher for the time being. This is a point, however, where a shorter term trader may want to try and scalp a few points if price begins a corrective phase. As price moved higher into point B, notice that the VPP broke its support line and actually made a lower high while price made a higher high, forming a negative divergence as price ran into the same resistance area as it encountered at point A. The negative divergence is marked by the thin solid lines at point B in the price plot and the plot of VPP. This was a stubborn resistance area that was difficult to overcome. The only problem with the candles at point B was that there was no real candle reversal pattern to trade off of. Price gapped higher into point B, forming an open window that was followed by a spinning top. This was not a classic harami because the candle colors were the same, but the black candle following the spinning top would have signaled at least a short-term reversal. One could have placed a trade here on the reversal with a protective buy stop just above the point B high. It is important to note that when there is no real discernable candle pattern but the indicator is diverging, proceed with caution and make sure that a protective stop order is in place should you decide to take the trade anyway.

Price chopped sideways before moving higher into point C, which was once again just below resistance, with the VPP moving even lower than it was at point B. The action in the VPP coupled with *another* evening star pattern at resistance tilted the scales sharply in favor of a profitable short trade. A short trade could have been entered as the candles confirmed the reversal with a protective buy stop just above the evening star at point C.

One thing to remember when viewing these examples is that in the real world every chart ends at the last candle. That may sound rather obvious, but what it means is that at point C in the previous example, on the day that the evening star candle formed there were no more candles to the right of it. The next day when price gapped lower, it was showtime. In other words, would you have had the courage to place the trade or not? Sure, in presenting these examples in hindsight it is easy to see that trade worked, but this is why stops should be used on every trade. In this business there are no guarantees, and since every chart you use in real time will have a hard right edge, a protective stop order may end up being your best friend—allowing you to live and trade another day. I cannot stress enough how important it is that you get a feel for various candle patterns and indicators before you venture out and begin trading. It is the same as a soldier going into battle without having any training in weapons handling and tactics. Patience is key, but when candlesticks and your indicators tell you it is time to act, do so without hesitation.

Summary

- Volume provides another way to measure the sentiment of the market.
- While volume analysis can be distorted by things like high-frequency trading, it is still a valuable tool when analyzed *over time.*
- Volume provides the fuel for price movement in the market.
- Changes in volume patterns can alert a trader that a change in price direction may be near.
- Volume moving averages allow a trader to analyze volume patterns over time.
- Indicators that combine price and volume can provide an extra level of analysis that ordinary price-based indicators lack.
- The money flow index is essentially the RSI indicator with a volume component added.
- The accumulation/distribution (AD) line shows longer term trends by combining price and volume data.
- The Chaikin AD oscillator is the difference between the 3- and 10-day moving averages of the AD line.
- Chaikin money flow is a centered oscillator derived from the past 21 days of the AD line divided by volume.
- The volume percent positive (VPP) indicator plots on a standardized scale that is not easily distorted by uneven volume totals.
- The VPP indicator allows for the easy plotting of support/resistance lines to show when volume trends may be changing.
- It is important that you get a feel for candle patterns and indicators before using them on live trades.
- When your indicators and candle patterns give you a trading signal, take it without hesitation.

QUIZ

1. **Volume is an often overlooked or dismissed component of market analysis.**
   A. True
   B. False

2. **Which indicator is best known as an RSI with a volume component added?**
   A. Chaikin money flow
   B. Money flow index
   C. Chaikin AD oscillator
   D. None of the above

3. **Which indicator is best for getting a longer term read on price and volume activity in market trends?**
   A. VPP indicator
   B. Chaikin AD oscillator
   C. AD line
   D. All of the above

4. **Which indicator is derived from the AD line?**
   A. Chaikin money flow
   B. Money flow index
   C. Chaikin AD oscillator
   D. Both A and C

5. **The weight of the evidence trading methodology is not as important when using volume based indicators.**
   A. True
   B. False

6. **Using volume-based indicators lessens the need for using protective stops on every trade.**
   A. True
   B. False

7. **Which tool allows a trader to analyze volume patterns over time?**
   A. Volume moving average
   B. Declining volume oscillator
   C. Chaikin AD oscillator
   D. None of the above

8. **When a volume-based indicator shows a divergence but there is no discernable candle reversal pattern, what should a trader do?**
   A. Make the trade anyway with little concern.
   B. Proceed cautiously and make sure a protective stop is in place if the trade is made.
   C. Not execute the trade at all.
   D. None of the above

9. What should a trader do when candle patterns and indicators are in agreement and give a trading signal?
   A. Wait and make sure the signal is correct.
   B. Use a protective stop order on the trade.
   C. Make the trade without hesitation.
   D. Both B and C

10. Short-term volume analysis can be distorted by things like high-frequency trading.
    A. True
    B. False

10

Weight of the Evidence—Trading Examples

Thus far we have covered a lot of ground. We have gone over candlestick formations and patterns; basic technical analysis such as support/resistance, retracement levels, moving averages, and trends; and looked at various price and momentum indicators. This chapter will explain how to put these pieces together to use the weight of the evidence methodology to find trades that have a higher probability of success.

CHAPTER OBJECTIVES

In this chapter you will

- Combine the concepts and methods presented in Chapters 1–9 to identify profitable trading opportunities
- Learn to trust your favorite indicators and candle formations
- Understand the synergy created by different analysis methods
- Know when to execute a trade and where to place your protective stop
- Have a mental checklist to review before each trade is executed

Trade Presentation Format

Each trade will have a hard right edge to the chart, meaning that as the candle pattern comes up, I will delete the remainder of the price data past that point to give you an idea of how uncertain trading can be with no data past "today." This will teach you to learn, understand, and trust your indicators and trading methodology. Always use protective stop orders on every trade, however, because no matter how thorough your preparation, your trades will not be successful every time. Using stops will save you from trying to rationalize holding a losing position when the price action is clearly telling you to exit the trade.

Each trade example will begin with a candlestick pattern. Then we will zoom out and look at the bigger picture such as support/resistance lines, retracement levels, and anything else that can tilt the odds of taking a trade in our favor.

Trade Example 1

In our first example we have a daily chart of Ford Motor Company (Fig. 10-1) that formed a classic bullish engulfing pattern (Chapter 4) on October 4, 2011, after a long decline. There is also a plot of a 20-day volume percent positive (VPP) (Chapter 9) below it. The first thing you will notice is that the VPP is showing significant positive divergence. As price continued to move lower, the VPP began making a series of higher lows, which showed that volume flows

FIGURE 10-1 • Bullish Engulfing Pattern: Ford Motor Company, Daily
Source: MetaStock

FIGURE 10-2 • Bullish Engulfing Pattern Support/Resistance: Ford Motor Company, Daily
Source: MetaStock

were higher on up days than down days in spite of the continued price decline. Is there more weight of the evidence data that we can gather to increase the odds of success for making the trade?

Now let's zoom out and see what else we can gather as weight of the evidence data that would tilt the odds of making a successful trade. In Fig. 10-2 the chart has been zoomed out to show price data beginning in July 2010. Notice that there are two lines marked A and B. These are support/resistance lines (also referred to as trend lines in Chapter 7) that were drawn based on past price reactions around them. These lines can act either as resistance when price approaches them from underneath or as support when price approaches them from above. Using lines like these can be very revealing in chart analysis. Never be afraid to connect price points to form these lines. Some of my charts have lines all over them, but when price encounters these lines, a reaction typically occurs that can help determine if an area will act as support or resistance when a candle pattern is formed. Remember a bullish reversal pattern formed at support has a higher chance of success because now there are two dynamics working in favor of a reversal—the reversal pattern and the support area.

If you look at line A you may think that was a line drawn in hindsight just to support the trade, but look closely at the line's origin. A split formed where there was a clear split between a price consolidation and a long white candle. Price actually gapped higher, and you can see the stark contrast in price behavior between the sideways consolidation and the explosion higher. That was an area to keep in mind when looking to draw new lines down the road. There was really no area to connect that split to until the inverted hammer that appeared on August 8, 2011. The reason for connecting the origin at point A with the inverted hammer was that price clearly bounced higher after the inverted hammer. That showed that there was sufficient buying energy there to at least cause a bounce. Again, the more lines you can create on a chart, the better prepared you will be.

Line B was drawn across the declining tops that formed August–September 2010. Line B also has a split or gap higher that shows a clear contrast between the consolidation phase and price explosion higher in September. Notice that lines A and B converge right at the point where the engulfing pattern formed. This showed solid support that caused a price reaction. These two lines provided more evidence of price support that would help tilt the odds in favor of a successful trade. There is even more evidence, however.

In Fig. 10-3, we zoom back in to get a closer look at more recent price action. Notice that there are also two external retracement levels (Chapter 7) as shown by the dotted lines and downward pointing arrows in the price plot. The first external retracement level is 161.8 percent of the August 8–16 price bounce. The second is a 127.2 percent external retracement of the September 23–27 bounce. Both of these levels are clustered close together, not only with each other but also with the extended support/resistance lines A and B that were drawn from earlier price points.

Finally, take a look at the VPP in the bottom pane. As price was making lower lows since early August, VPP was making higher lows. This showed that volume

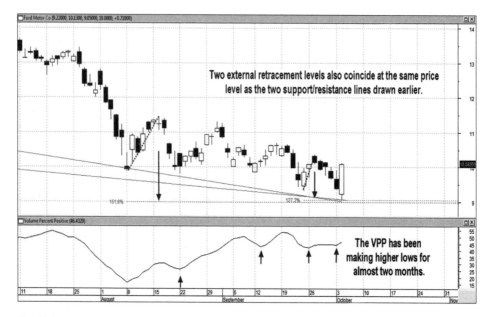

FIGURE 10-3 • Bullish Engulfing Pattern Evidence: Ford Motor Company, Daily
Source: MetaStock

on up days was coming in stronger than volume on down days—a sign of share accumulation. Putting everything together, we have

1. A bullish engulfing pattern
2. At support as shown by two separate support resistance lines drawn from earlier price points
3. At two external retracement levels that coincide also with the support/resistance lines
4. With a rising VPP, which made higher lows as price continued to make lower lows

This was a trade that should have been taken because of the compelling evidence gathered to back up the candle reversal pattern. A trade could have been placed when the reversal was confirmed as price closed higher the day following the engulfing candle. One final piece of evidence was the break of the down-sloping resistance line that connected the declining tops in August and September. The confirmation in the form of a higher close not only validated the engulfing pattern, but it also broke through short-term resistance, which provided evidence that a price reversal was under way. A protective sell stop should have been just below the low of the engulfing candle (Fig. 10-4).

Every chart tells a story. The more information you can gather about past behavior and where traders tend to react, the better chance you will have at being in synch with the market and able to make profitable trades.

FIGURE 10-4 • Bullish Engulfing Pattern Trade: Ford Motor Company, Daily
Source: MetaStock

Trade Example 2

The next example is a bearish engulfing pattern reversal on a daily chart of Wynn Resorts Inc. (Fig. 10-5) that formed on July 19, 2011. A 14-day RSI (Chapter 8) is shown below the price plot. Would this be a good trade to take? Let's once again assess the weight of the evidence.

FIGURE 10-5 • Bearish Engulfing Pattern: Wynn Resorts Inc., Daily
Source: MetaStock

Figure 10-6 shows a longer term view of Wynn Resorts, and one thing you will notice rather quickly is that we can invoke one of the longer term patterns presented in Chapter 6. The principle of *eight new price lines*, or *shinne hatte*, is governed by the philosophy that one should take profits after eight new price highs are set. If you look at the chart, there are clearly eight new price highs during the move from the March 2009 low. There are also two support/resistance lines, labeled A and B, as well as an external retracement level that comes in at the level in which the bearish engulfing pattern formed.

Line A is a simple line that connects the tops between November 2010 and May 2011. Notice how it comes in contact with the area where the bearish engulfing pattern formed. Line B connects the March and May lows before also extending up into the area where the bearish engulfing pattern formed. These two lines come together to form a rather strong barrier to price advances, which should provide more validation for the bearish engulfing pattern.

FIGURE 10-6 • Bearish Engulfing Pattern Zoom Out: Wynn Resorts Inc., Daily
Source: MetaStock

Zooming in closer to more recent action in Fig. 10-7, you get a closer look at line B to see its origin and the points to which it is connected. The fact that price bounced higher in mid-May was reason enough to draw a line connecting that to the earlier low, but also notice how price clung to the line following the bounce higher. Price briefly traded on both sides of the line while making contact with it for eight straight days before breaking lower in early June. That shows the importance of that line to price reactions. Finally, take a look just to the left of the bearish engulfing pattern. A long white candle formed that ended right at line B before price chopped sideways for a few days. That candle is marked with an upward pointing black arrow on the chart.

There is also a retracement level that has come into play here as well. It is the 161.8 percent external retracement from the May high to the June low. This was an important range because it was the final correction of any magnitude before price pushed out to its next high. The range that was retraced is marked with a dotted line with an upward pointing arrow to the retracement level. The final piece of evidence is the negative divergence that formed between price and the RSI. Notice that price made a higher high while the RSI made a lower high. This showed a loss of momentum as price pushed into its final high where the engulfing pattern formed. The divergent action between price and the RSI is marked by a dotted line over the subsequent highs in price and the corresponding highs in the RSI.

FIGURE 10-7 • Bearish Engulfing Pattern Retracement and Divergence: Wynn Resorts Inc., Daily
Source: MetaStock

When you see the confluence of the external retracement plus the crossing of lines A and B, along with the negative divergence on the RSI that shows weakening momentum, that is formidable resistance. The fact that the bearish engulfing pattern formed at this level adds more strength to the pattern, as price broke through these levels only to reverse lower and close below them on the engulfing day. This is known as a failure at resistance and should provide compelling evidence that a short trade should be taken, or at the very least, long positions should be exited. So let's sum up our weight of the evidence here. We have

1. A bearish engulfing pattern
2. Formed at resistance formed by the confluence of lines A and B
3. At a 161.8 percent external retracement level
4. With a negative divergence between price and the RSI
5. After eight new price highs were made in the advance

The day following the engulfing candle provided confirmation of the reversal as price closed lower on the day. A short trade could have been placed prior to the close of that day when it looked obvious that price would close lower, but there would also be no harm in waiting for price to officially close lower and sell short the next day just after the open. Price chopped sideways for four days before finally breaking sharply lower. Figure 10-8 shows the trade, stop placement, and subsequent price action.

FIGURE 10-8 • Bearish Engulfing Pattern Trade: Wynn Resorts Inc., Daily
Source: MetaStock

There is one final point to be made regarding this trade, however, and that is the distance between the trade entry price ($160) and the high of the engulfing candle ($172). It pays to always know the risk you are taking on when entering a trade. In this case, the risk would have been around 7 percent. Make sure that you can afford to lose that much if your protective buy stop is touched. If the loss would be too great, you would be better served to wait for a trading opportunity with less risk. While some reversal patterns can look rather spectacular on a price chart, do not let the excitement suck you into a trade where you cannot afford to lose the amount between your entry price and your protective stop price.

Still Struggling?

Not all trades will be successful.

A successful trade is one that moves a trader into a position to make a profit. Whether the trades were actually successful is irrelevant for the purposes of these examples. You will have times where no matter how compelling the evidence in favor of the trade, it just simply moves against you. I have had many trades like this, and so will you. Such is the nature of the markets. With regard to unsuccessful trades, try to find a point of analysis that you may have missed in building your weight of the evidence. This will help prevent making the same mistake in the future. In some cases you may not be able to find a flaw in your analysis. That is OK too. The point here is that by using stops a losing trade is booked and you move on, ready to fight another day. Unless you have discovered a flaw in your analysis, do not be afraid to try the same trade on the same stock/ETF/futures contract if you have the same setup. Do your homework, and hone your craft.

Trade Example 3

The third example is a dark cloud cover pattern that appeared on May 13, 2011, on the daily chart of Oracle Corp. (Fig. 10-9). The chart also has a plot of a 20-day moving average oscillator (MAO) (Chapter 7). Notice in this case that the dark cloud cover forms at a secondary high just below the previous high. Trade setups like these are worth a serious look as the formation of a reversal pattern just below resistance shows that sellers are trying to gain control of the trend.

Next let's zoom out to see what other evidence we can gather in support of taking this trade. Figure 10-10 has a longer term view so we can get an idea how

FIGURE 10-9 • Dark Cloud Cover: Oracle Corp., Daily

Source: MetaStock

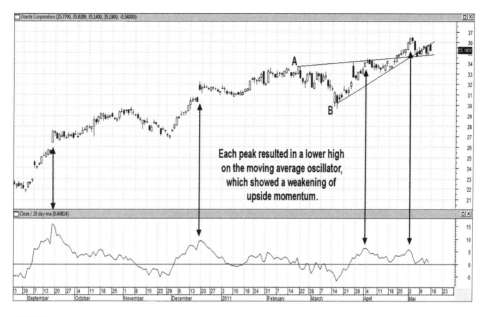

FIGURE 10-10 • Dark Cloud Cover Zoom Out: Oracle Corp., Daily
Source: MetaStock

this trade is setting up. First notice the double-sided arrows drawn from price peaks to MAO peaks. Each time price made a higher high, the MAO made a lower high. This shows diminishing upside momentum as the trend matures. Remember the 20-day MAO is merely the difference between the closing price and a simple 20-day moving average. The first peak was made when price exploded higher in September 2010 as the new uptrend began. As price made subsequent peaks in December 2010, March 2011, and May 2011, the price explosion higher was weaker in relation to the 20-day moving average as it did not pull as far away. This is normal behavior as trends develop and mature because the 20-day moving average is now trending higher with price, so the gaps are not as wide. There are also two lines drawn on the chart labeled A and B. Again, these represent levels where we can gauge support and resistance to help us determine what price is likely to do in order for the trade to be successful. Line A is drawn across the February and March 2011 tops while line B is an uptrend line drawn off of the mid-March low.

Now let's take a closer look at the price action around the trade so you can see where lines A and B come into play in Fig. 10-11. First notice how line A is drawn across the tops in February and March, and when extended it also served as support at point C. The horizontal line off of point C has also been added as a new support area due to the price bounce off of line A. Line B was drawn off of the mid-March low and connected lower shadows as well as the bottom of the real body of the small white candle on April 19. When extended, this line

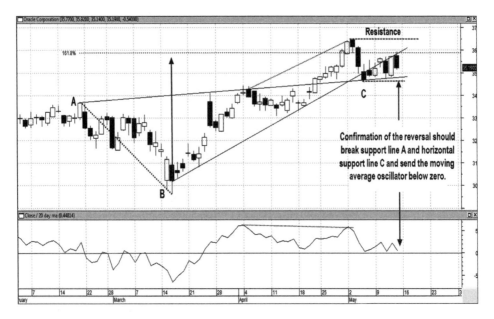

FIGURE 10-11 • Dark Cloud Cover Support/Resistance: Oracle Corp., Daily
Source: MetaStock

became resistance later after price peaked on May 3 and sold off. Notice all the touches of line B following the bounce higher at point C. This is also a very important line. In this combination of lines, we have line B providing overhead resistance, with lines A and C providing support. The key takeaway from this is that a confirmation of the dark cloud cover reversal could also serve to break two levels of support (lines A and C) as well as push the MAO below its zero line, which would mean that price closed below its 20-day moving average—another bearish development.

A 161.8 percent external retracement level has been added, which was drawn off of the February–March decline (the dotted line) with an upward-pointing arrow drawn up to the retracement level. There is also the horizontal resistance line drawn off of the May 3 high. The fact that the dark cloud cover formed just below this resistance level constituted a failure at resistance, which is a bearish development. That same failure with the 161.8 percent external retracement level added to it painted an even more bearish picture. Yet one more piece of evidence is the negative divergence between the MAO and price between the late March and early May highs. Price made a noticeably higher high while the MAO made a slightly lower high—again showing weakening upside momentum in price movement.

So let's see what evidence exists for taking this trade. We have

1. A dark cloud cover pattern
2. Just below resistance at the prior high and resistance from line B

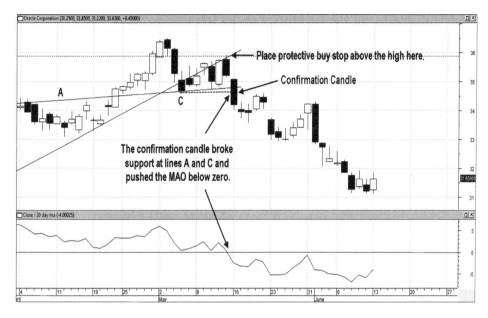

FIGURE 10-12 • Dark Cloud Cover Trade: Oracle Corp., Daily
Source: MetaStock

3. A negative divergence between price and the MAO

4. A 161.8 percent external retracement of the February–March decline as a resistance level

5. A confirmation of the dark cloud cover reversal should be enough to break support and push the MAO below its zero line

Now let's take a look at how the trade worked out (Fig. 10-12). The very next day the confirmation candle broke support at lines A and C, and the MAO pushed below zero, a strong signal that there was some real downside momentum building here. A short trade could have been placed at or near the closing price on the confirmation day (34.18), or just after the open the following day (34.03). A protective buy stop should have been placed just above the high of the dark cloud cover. Price then tumbled to the 31 area by mid-June.

The examples shown were all trades that would have generated profits. I know that some of you are saying that these trades were "cherry-picked" to show success with these methodologies. That is a true statement. That is exactly how you should trade as well. Look for at least three pieces of evidence from your indicators, support/resistance levels, and candle patterns. The weight of the evidence methodology will allow you to filter trades that have a higher chance of profit. Never wing it, and never take a trade "just because." Always have sound reasoning backed up by evidence that the trade is setting up favorably.

Another rule to always adhere to is *never* move your stop unless it is in the direction of the trade to trail profits and lock in gains. Do not ever move your stop further away from price just to "give it more room." Your stop was set at a specific place for a reason. If the stop is hit, then it is time to exit the trade, pure and simple. That doesn't mean you can't make the same trade at a similar price level if another setup takes place, but if your stop order is touched and executed, move to the sidelines and wait for the next opportunity.

Trader's Checklist

Understanding the tools presented here and using them are only half the battle. In order to become a successful trader, you must also be prepared mentally to do battle with the markets every day. Here is a checklist of six points to remember as you begin your trading journey.

1. **Guard against fear and greed.** Never get caught up in the emotions of the masses. Let your own analysis dictate your actions. Always assess what is; do not get caught up in the successes or failures of others.

2. **Be patient.** Always wait for confirmation of a reversal or continuation pattern. Assuming that a pattern will resolve itself in a certain way will lead to unnecessary losses.

3. **Never be influenced by news.** Following CNBC and other all day market news sources can get you caught up in intra-day hype. Never be distracted by the "why," only concentrate on the "what." In other words price action itself is king. Don't worry about the reasons that others put on price movement to try and rationalize it.

4. **The market is never wrong.** Even if you have the best setup ever and the market moves against you—get out if your stop price is touched. The market doesn't care about your opinion—it is made up of the collective will of *all* traders.

5. **Never waver in your execution.** When the weight of the evidence says it is time to pull the trigger, do so without hesitation.

6. **Always use stops.** I can't stress this enough. Using stops will prevent small losses from snowballing into crippling ones. You will not be profitable on every trade no matter how thorough your preparation. Do not become a "buy and holder" because the trade moved against you. If your stop price is touched, get out and wait for the next opportunity when your weight of the evidence aligns once again.

Summary

- Always use a weight of the evidence methodology to gather information before placing trades.
- Learn the characteristics of the indicators you choose to use.

- Support/resistance lines can typically be drawn in many places on charts. Always look for them.
- Retracement levels can provide extra support/resistance areas that other methods may miss.
- Always remember and try to apply other strategies such as eight new price lines as shown in the Wynn Resorts example.
- Knowing the technical side is only half the battle. Always be in control of your emotions.
- Never hesitate when the weight of the evidence shows that it is time to place a trade.
- Always use stops on every trade.

QUIZ

1. When trading using indicators, it doesn't matter which you choose to use since they are all the same.
   A. True
   B. False

2. How many pieces of evidence should a trader have at minimum before placing a trade?
   A. One
   B. Two
   C. Three
   D. Four

3. If an indicator shows a divergence with price
   A. That is enough reason to enter a trade
   B. It should simply be one piece of the weight of the evidence
   C. One can assume that the trade will develop favorably
   D. None of the above

4. Knowing the technical side of trading is enough to become a successful trader.
   A. True
   B. False

5. Support and resistance can be measured by
   A. Support/resistance lines
   B. Internal retracement levels
   C. External retracement levels
   D. All of the above

6. When trading you must protect yourself from
   A. Fear
   B. Greed
   C. Being influenced by the news
   D. All of the above

7. When the weight of the evidence triggers a trading signal, it is always best to take your time and make sure it is accurate.
   A. True
   B. False

8. A reversal pattern at prior resistance is known as a
   A. Failure at resistance
   B. Missed opportunity
   C. Guaranteed winning trade
   D. None of the above

9. **When drawing support/resistance lines, it is best to connect**
   A. Only highs
   B. All prior inflection points where price reacted
   C. Only horizontal points
   D. Only lows

10. **Protective stop orders should be used on every trade.**
    A. True
    B. False

Conclusion

A lot of material has been covered in the previous pages to try and give you a broad spectrum of candlestick patterns, the theories behind them, and the conceptual foundation off of which they were developed. In addition, I have shown a basic sampling of other tools that are available to help you make more informed trading decisions. While I have not given you a hard and fast system that will allow you to plug in and go, you now have the basic foundation to allow you to explore the options available and to develop a deeper understanding of trading and how to do it successfully.

Being a successful trader takes time and patience. Books that hand you a canned trading system are not really helping you develop your potential as a trader. Every trading system has periods when it does not work very well because the market is always changing. If you are simply given a canned trading system and it hits a rough period, what do you do? With a broad, basic understanding of candlesticks and technical analysis, you will have the confidence to try new ideas. Remember, if no one had thought outside the box previously, technical analysis would not exist in its present form. Use the work of others as a springboard to test your own ideas and extend your own understanding.

This book covered the more common candle patterns, or those that occur with great frequency. There are many other candle patterns that were discovered and developed by Greg Morris, who is a true pioneer in this area. I would highly recommend picking up a copy of *Candlestick Charting Explained*, originally written in 1993 and now in its third edition. That book is an invaluable reference to candle patterns. As I stated earlier, *Martin Pring on Market Momentum* is a great book for developing your understanding of momentum indicators and their uses. I would also recommend *All About Technical Analysis* by Connie Brown. In fact, any book written by Connie is a great addition to your trading library as she is one of the best teachers of technical analysis I have ever read.

Also, virtually all of the examples in this book were shown in the daily time frame. Candlestick charting was developed for use in the daily time frame so that traders would have a chance to interpret news they received in off-hours when the markets were closed. It was designed to capture trader reactions and interpretations on a daily basis. That dynamic is not as prevalent when using candlesticks for intra-day or weekly trading. That does not mean they cannot be used in those time frames, however. The extra information given by candlestick charting will work in any time frame, so there was no point in showing a bunch of examples in different time frames. A broad sampling of material needed to be covered, and the concepts are transferable to other time frames.

Trading the markets today is more difficult than ever because of the intervention of world banks and the seemingly endless stream of bailouts being handed to mismanaged companies and nations. The extra liquidity sloshing around in the markets can sometimes distort reality. By using a sound trading methodology, however, you can gain a deeper understanding of what price is *likely* to do, thus tilting the odds in your favor of making a successful trade.

Once you have assembled the tools you will use, remember to always use a weight of the evidence methodology for selecting and entering trades. When the weight of the evidence tells you it is time to place a trade, do so unwaveringly and without hesitation. Always remember that human emotions can deceive a trader and can cloud otherwise sound judgment. Never get caught up in news stories, rumors, or how much money someone else is making. Choose your indicators and trust them implicitly. Also remember to always use stops. They will serve you well because no matter how thorough your analysis, the market is always right. As the old saying goes, if you give a man a fish, he will eat for a day, but if you teach him how to fish, he will eat for a lifetime. I have given you the materials to build your own fishing pole. Never stop looking for new and better ways to use it. You should never have to settle for the Wall Street fraud of buy and hold again.

Best of luck and happy trading!

Final Exam

1. Technical analysis is used for
   A. Predicting price movement
   B. Guaranteeing that a trade will be successful
   C. Determining what price is likely to do
   D. All of the above

2. What is the purpose of shadows in candlestick construction?
   A. To show the time of day that a trade was made
   B. To show the extreme high and low prices of the day
   C. To create specific candlestick patterns
   D. None of the above

3. Which of Sakata's strategies means "buy, sell, and rest"?
   A. Three gaps   B. Three methods
   C. Three soldiers   D. Three rivers

4. Moving averages are used to reflect
   A. Support/resistance areas   B. Trends
   C. Both A and B   D. None of the above

5. Which candle type has opening and closing prices that are virtually equal?
   A. Marubozu   B. Spinning Top
   C. Tasuki   D. Doji

6. Candlestick charting is based on the work of
   A. Ichiro Sakata   B. Charles Dow
   C. Steve Nison   D. Munehisa Honma

7. Stepping aside during times of market weakness is
   A. A recipe for disaster
   B. Frowned upon by Wall Street and the financial media
   C. An important way to accumulate wealth
   D. Both B and C

8. The writings of Charles Dow form the basis of Western technical analysis
   A. True   B. False

9. A change in price direction is virtually guaranteed by
   A. A valid candlestick reversal pattern
   B. A trend line violation
   C. A star pattern
   D. There is nothing that guarantees a change in price direction

10. Continuation patterns represent
    A. Periods of high emotion
    B. Periods of rest, or consolidation, in an existing trend
    C. Periods when trading should be avoided
    D. Periods when trading opportunities have been missed

11. What number is prevalent in Sakata's strategies?
    A. One   B. Two
    C. Three   D. Seven

12. If price breaks above resistance, the broken resistance then becomes
    A. Support   B. Even stronger resistance
    C. A top   D. None of the above

13. Which moving average types are most commonly used in the MACD indicator?
    A. Weighted   B. Triangular
    C. Simple   D. Exponential

14. Which reversal pattern signals that an uptrend may be ready to reverse lower?
    A. Morning Star   B. Tasuki Gap
    C. Suzuki Reversal   D. Dark Cloud Cover

15. Gaps are known as what in candlestick trading?
    A. Harami   B. Doji
    C. Windows   D. Tasuki Lines

16. Which continuation pattern consists of consecutive candles that have the same opening price but move in the opposite direction?
    A. Meeting lines   B. In-neck lines
    C. Separating lines   D. On-neck lines

17. The formation of a valid candlestick reversal pattern means
    A. A trader should always wait for price to confirm the reversal
    B. A trader need not wait for completion of the pattern to make the most possible profit
    C. Stops should always be used regardless of the pattern
    D. Both A and C

18. Which statement is true regarding windows?
    A. A rising window provides support while a falling window provides resistance.
    B. Windows show periods of high emotion.
    C. Their formation provides a clear level for stop placement.
    D. All of the above

19. Marubozu are classified by
    A. A. The absence of an upper and/or lower shadow
    B. A small real body
    C. Long shadows at either end
    D. None of the above

20. Short-term volume analysis can be distorted by things like high-frequency trading.
    A. True   B. False

21. Successful traders must always
    A. Have a gift of knowing which trades will be successful in advance
    B. Have access to instantaneous data
    C. React to the latest news
    D. Remain objective

22. Which reversal pattern is NOT valid in an uptrend?
    A. Evening star   B. Dark cloud cover
    C. Morning star   D. Hanging man

23. Volume is used to measure
    A. The number of shares or contracts that changed hands during the trading day
    B. The conviction level among traders
    C. The amount of greed in the market
    D. Both A and B

24. Candlestick reversal patterns are just as reliable in sideways or choppy markets as they are in trending markets.
    A. True   B. False

25. A piercing line is a valid reversal pattern in a uptrend.
    A. True   B. False

26. A tasuki line consists of
   A. A line following a white candle that opens in the real body of the white candle and closes below its low
   B. An open window followed by a black candle
   C. A "line in the sand" that differentiates between trends
   D. All of the above

27. Trend lines can be drawn through meaningful price movement areas on a chart, not just connecting major highs and lows.
   A. True   B. False

28. Trader indecision is best represented by
   A. A small real body
   B. An open window
   C. A long lower shadow
   D. None of the above

29. A divergence between a momentum indicator and price action means
   A. Take the trade quicky as price will change direction
   B. A stop need not be used on the trade
   C. It is merely one piece of evidence that a change in price direction may be near
   D. Both A and B

30. Which reversal pattern is NOT a derivative of the three soldiers?
   A. Deliberation
   B. Advance block
   C. Three black crows
   D. Three mountains

31. Which momentum indicator measures the closing price against the high/low range for the period?
   A. RSI   B. Rate of change
   C. Stochastic   D. MACD

32. When learning candlestick reversal patterns it is best to understand
   A. The psychology behind the pattern
   B. Trend direction when identifying the patterns
   C. That they reflect a short-term change in trader psychology
   D. All of the above

33. Which pattern is NOT a failed piercing line or dark cloud cover pattern?
   A. Harami   B. On-neck line
   C. Thrusting pattern   D. In-neck line

34. Price trend is not important when trading continuation patterns
   A. True   B. False

35. Which candle pattern most resembles a *rounded* reversal in Western technical analysis?
    A. Dumpling top or bottom
    B. Gapping play
    C. Tower top or bottom
    D. None of the above

36. Which of the following is a valid type of gap?
    A. Suzuki   B. Samurai
    C. Explosion   D. Runaway

37. One thing successful traders must do is
    A. Pay attention to the profits of others in order to stay ahead of the crowd
    B. Treat it as a business
    C. Have a lot of "connections" in the industry
    D. Find the best trading chat rooms

38. What two types of risk are not addressed by the buy-and-hold methodology?
    A. Diversification and overlay
    B. Drawdown and lost opportunity
    C. Conservative and excessive
    D. None of the above

39. Which charting style only uses the closing price in its construction?
    A. Line
    B. Point and figure
    C. Candlestick
    D. Bar

40. Which continuation pattern consists of a sharp price move followed by three days of rest?
    A. Tasuki gap
    B. Separating lines
    C. Thrusting line
    D. Rising or falling three methods

41. One concept to be aware of when choosing a moving average length is
    A. Trend line fit
    B. The certainty of support/resistance areas
    C. Reversal probability
    D. Lag

42. The size and color of a real body represents the relationship between
    A. The closing prices of the past two candles
    B. Low and closing prices
    C. High and closing prices
    D. Opening and closing prices

43. What are some of the advantages of candlestick charts over bar charts?
    A. Readability
    B. Quicker interpretation of market psychology
    C. Specific patterns give insight into market sentiment
    D. All of the above

44. Whipsaw signals are not a concern that one needs to be aware of when using momentum indicators.
    A. True
    B. False

45. Fear and greed are good emotions for a trader to have at all times.
    A. True
    B. False

46. Which of these patterns penetrates the real body of the previous candle?
    A. Piercing line
    B. Dark cloud cover
    C. Thrusting pattern
    D. All of the above

47. When the weight of the evidence gives a trading signal the trader should
    A. Make the trade without hesitation
    B. Use a protective stop order on the trade
    C. Consult with trusted contacts to verify the signal
    D. Both A and B

48. A gravestone doji has
    A. A long upper shadow
    B. A long shadow at both ends
    C. A long lower shadow
    D. None of the above

49. A doji is most meaningful
    A. In a sideways or choppy market
    B. Only in downtrends
    C. Only in uptrends
    D. In a trending market regardless of direction

50. Which doji typically has very small upper and lower shadows?
    A. Gravestone doji
    B. Dragonfly doji
    C. Long-legged doji
    D. Evening star doji

Answers to Quizzes and Final Exam

Chapter 1	Chapter 3	Chapter 5	Chapter 7
1. A	1. A	1. B	1. A
2. B	2. C	2. C	2. B
3. C	3. A	3. A	3. A
4. C	4. A	4. D	4. C
5. D	5. D	5. C	5. D
6. D	6. D	6. D	6. C
7. C	7. C	7. C	7. D
8. B	8. D	8. D	8. B
9. A	9. C	9. D	9. A
10. C	10. A	10. B	10. C

Chapter 2	Chapter 4	Chapter 6	Chapter 8
1. D	1. B	1. B	1. C
2. B	2. A	2. C	2. B
3. C	3. C	3. C	3. B
4. D	4. D	4. A	4. A
5. B	5. D	5. B	5. D
6. C	6. C	6. B	6. D
7. D	7. C	7. A	7. C
8. C	8. C	8. B	8. A
9. D	9. B	9. D	9. B
10. C	10. A	10. D	10. B

Chapter 9	7. B	13. D	32. D
1. A	8. A	14. D	33. A
2. B	9. B	15. C	34. B
3. C	10. A	16. C	35. A
4. D		17. D	36. D
5. B	Final Exam	18. D	37. B
6. B	Answers	19. A	38. B
7. A	1. C	20. A	39. A
8. B	2. B	21. D	40. D
9. D	3. B	22. C	41. D
10. A	4. C	23. D	42. D
	5. D	24. B	43. D
Chapter 10	6. D	25. B	44. B
1. B	7. D	26. A	45. B
2. C	8. A	27. A	46. D
3. B	9. D	28. A	47. D
4. B	10. B	29. C	48. A
5. D	11. C	30. D	49. D
6. D	12. A	31. C	50. D

Index

Abandoned babies, 53
Abandoned baby bottom, 54
Abandoned baby top, 54
Accumulation/distribution line (AD line), 195–198
Achelis, Steven, 161
ADO (Chaikin AD oscillator), 198
Advance block pattern (three soldiers), 111
AFLAC Inc. (bullish harami), 58–59
AK Steel Holding Corp. (bullish belt hold), 61
Alcoa Inc. (bearish belt hold), 62
Altria Group Inc. (stochastic trends), 173
Amazon.com Inc.
  breakaway gap, 152
  high price gapping play, 123–124
  three upside gaps, 109
American Express Co.
  MACD, 161–162
  moving average oscillator smoothed, 160–161
  moving average oscillator whipsaws, 159–160
Ameriprise Financial Inc.
  ROC trade, 166
  ROC trend, 165
Amgen Inc. (external retracement levels), 148–149
Apollo Group Inc. (ROC trends), 168
Apple Inc.
  eight new price lines, 125

  runaway gap, 152–153
  volume patterns, 189
Arch Coal Inc. (shooting star), 55
AT&T Inc. (rising three method), 98

Baidu Inc. (hammer pattern), 39
Banded oscillators, 158–159, 170
Bank of America Corp.
  20-day and 10-day moving averages, 135–136
  separating lines, 86
Bar chart lines, candlestick lines vs., 24
Bar charts, 18, 24
Barrick Gold Corp. (support area), 140
BB&T Corp. (bearish harami), 58–59
Bearish engulfing pattern, 44–45
Bearish engulfing pattern combined, 44
Bearish engulfing pattern example, 219
Bearish in-neck lines, 88–90
Bearish on-neck lines, 92–93
Bearish separating lines, 87
Bearish thrusting lines, 94–95
Belt hold lines, 60–62
Black marubozu, 27
Black sanpei (*see* Three black crows), 111
Boeing Co. (upside gap two crows), 67–68
Bohraku (*see* Low price gapping plays)
Bohtoh (*see* High price gapping plays
Breakaway gaps, 152

Broken support becoming resistance, 140–50
Bullish engulfing pattern, 41–44
Bullish engulfing pattern example, 216
Bullish in-neck lines, 88–90
Bullish on-neck lines, 91–92
Bullish separating lines, 85–87
Bullish thrusting lines, 94
Buy-and-hold methodology, 1–4

Candlestick charting, history of, 6–7
Candlestick charts
  bar charts vs., 24
  data points for, 24
Candlestick continuation patterns.
    (see Continuation patterns)
Candlestick lines, 24
Candlestick reversal patterns (see Reversal
    patterns)
Candle types, 26
  long candles, 26
  marubozu, 28
  short candles, 27
Caterpillar Inc. (MACD trades), 162–163
CBL & Associates Properties Inc.
    (thrusting lines), 94
Centered oscillators, 158
Chaikin AD oscillator (ADO), 198–200
Chaikin, Marc, 195
Chaikin money flow (CMF), 200–202
Channels, 138
Charting styles
  bar chart, 18
  line chart, 16
  point and figure chart, 17
Chart (term), 15
Checklist, trader's, 224
Choppy markets, 27
Cisco Systems Inc. (bearish meeting lines), 66
Citigroup, Inc.
  HLV indicator, 179–180
  HLV indicator trade, 181
  morning star, 50–51
Closing marubozu, 28
Closing prices, relationship between opening
    and, 7
CMF (Chaikin money flow), 202

Coca-Cola Company
  20-day moving average, 132–133
  20-day moving average with indicator,
    133–134
  20-day moving average with indicator
    divergence, 134–135
Color
  candlestick, 7, 18
  of body, 24
Common gaps, 152
CONSOL Energy Inc. (three white soldiers), 63
Consumer Staples Select Sector SPDR ETF
    (tweezer top), 121
Continuation patterns, 101
  advantage of identifying/trading with, 80
  neck and thrusting lines as, 96
  neck lines, 93
  rising and falling three methods, 99
  separating lines, 88
  thrusting lines, 96
  windows, 85
Conviction (among traders), 26
Corrections (see Retracements)
Counterattack lines, 65–66
CSX Corp.
  common gaps, 151
  in-neck lines, 89
Cummins Inc. (RSI trends), 174–175

%D line, 169
Dark cloud cover, 47–49
Dark cloud cover combined, 48
Dark cloud cover example, 224
Day trading, 3
Deliberation (three soldiers), 111–112
Doji, 29–30
  dragonfly, 32
  gravestone, 31
  long-legged, 30–31
Doji candle, 13
Doji stars, 54
Dow, Charles, 11
Dow Jones Industrial Average, 11,
    105–106
Downside gap three method, 113–114
Downside tasuki gap, 83

Downtrends, 130, 139
Dow Theory, 11
Dragonfly doji, 32
Drawdown, 14
Dumpling tops, 118–120
Dun & Bradstreet Corp. (three outside
    down), 73

eBay Inc. (downside gap three method), 114
Eight new price lines, 125–126, 216
Engulfing patterns, 41–45 (*See also* Bearish
    engulfing pattern; Bullish engulfing pattern)
European Central Bank, 143
Evening star, 53, 162
Exhaustion gaps, 151, 153–154
Expedia Inc.
    harami cross, 60
    on-neck lines, 91–92
Exponential moving average, 132
External retracements, 149
Exxon Mobil Corp.
    MACD continuation, 163–164
    price trends, 130–131
    ten-minute bars, 131–132

Falling windows, 19, 80
Fear, 5, 224
Federal Reserve, 18
FedEx Corp.
    in-neck lines, 90
    internal retracement levels, 146–147
Fibonacci series, 146
Financial Select Sector SPDR ETF
    broken support now resistance, 141
    tower top, 116–117
First Solar Inc. (three down gaps),
    109–110
FLIR Systems Inc. (retracement cluster),
    149–150
Flowserve Corp.
    MFI, 193–194
    MFI trade, 193–194
    volume patterns, 190–191
Ford Motor Company
    bullish engulfing pattern, 212
    bullish engulfing pattern evidence, 214

bullish engulfing pattern support/resistance,
    213
bullish engulfing pattern trade, 215
Freeport McMoRan Copper and Gold Inc.
    (bullish engulfing pattern), 42–43
Fry pan bottoms, 118–120
Fundamental analysis, technical analysis vs.,
    12, 15

Gapping plays, 123–125
Gaps, 18, 150–154
    breakaway, 152
    common, 151
    exhaustion, 153–154
    runaway, 152–153
Gold rush, 5
Google, Inc., 12–14
    bar chart for, 18
    candlestick chart for, 19
    dumpling top, 119
    falling three method, 99
    point and figure chart for, 17
    three black crows, 64–65
Gravestone doji, 31
Greed, 5, 224
Guggenheim Solar ETF
    bearing engulfing pattern, 44–45
    doji morning star, 53–54

Hammer pattern, 38–40
Hanging man pattern, 40–41
Harami, 57–60
Head and shoulders reversal pattern, 105
Herd (term), 5
High/low volatility (HLV) indicator, 178–184
High price gapping plays, 123
History of candlestick charting, 7
HLV (*see* High/low volatility indicator)
Home Depot Inc.
    on-neck lines, 92–93
    stochastic trades, 170, 172
Honeywell International Inc.
    AD line, 196
    ADO trade, 198
    AD trade, 196–197
Honma constitution (*see* Sakata's strategies)

Honma, Munehisa, 7, 104
Horizontal lines and bands, 144

Identical three crows, 113
Illiquidity, 190
Indecision (among buyers), 26
Industrial Select Sector SPDR ETF
    channels, 138–139
    tweezer bottom, 122
Inflation, S&P 500 Index and, 2
In-neck lines, 88–91
In-neck lines combined, 89
Intel Corp.
    evening star, 52
    upside gap three method, 114
Internal retracements, 148
International Paper Co. (RSI characteristics),
    176
Internet stocks, 4
Inverted hammer, 54–56
Inverted three Buddha, 107
iShares Barclays 7-10 Year Treasury Bond ETF
    (three black crows), 111–112
iShares Barclays 20+ Year Treasury Bond ETF
    deliberation, 111–112
    three soldiers, 110
    upside tasuki gap, 84
iShares MSCI Emerging Markets ETF
    (three soldiers), 109

%K line, 169
KB Home (ADO trade), 199
Kenuki (see Tweezer tops and tweezer bottoms)
KLA-Tencor Corp. (three mountains),
    105–106

L3 Communications Holdings Inc.
    (three inside up), 70
Lag, 135
Lane, George, 169
Length
    of real body, 24
    of shadow, 25
Leonard of Pisa, 146
Light Sweet Crude Oil (tower bottom),
    117–118

Line charts, 16
Liquidity, low, 190
Long candles, 26
Longer term candle patterns, 126
    dumpling tops and fry pan bottoms, 120
    eight new price lines, 126
    gapping plays, 125
    tower tops and tower bottoms, 118
    tweezer tops and tweezer bottoms, 123
Long-legged doji, 30–31
Loss, fear of, 5
Lost opportunity, risk of, 14
Lower shadow, 25
Low liquidity, 190
Low price gapping plays, 123

MACD, 159–164, 178
MAO (moving average oscillator), 220
Market conditions, reversal patterns and, 57
Market pullbacks, 143
Market timing, 3
Market Vectors Steel ETF (thrusting lines), 95
Martin Pring on Market Momentum (Martin
    Pring), 184
Marubozu lines, 28
Marubozu (term), 27
Meeting lines, 65–67
MFI (see Money flow index)
Microsoft Corp. (inverted hammer), 56
Mindset, trader, 30
Momentum indicators, 157–185
    choosing appropriate, 178
    high/low volatility indicator, 184
    limitations of, 158
    oscillators, 158–178
    use of, 157
Money flow index (MFI), 193–195
Morning star, 51
Morris, Greg, 69
Moving average oscillator (MAO), 178, 220
Moving average oscillator smoothed, 160–161
Moving average oscillator whipsaws,
    159–160
Moving averages, 136
    and support/resistance, 145
    simple vs. exponential, 132

Nabezoko (*see* Dumpling tops; Fry pan bottoms)
Neck lines, 88–93, 96
Neutral trends, 132
Newmont Mining Corp. (three outside up), 72
News, 224
NVIDIA Corp.
    dark cloud cover, 48–49
    rising and falling windows, 80–81
NYMEX Crude Oil Futures (three rivers), 108
NYSE Composite Index (three rivers), 107

Objectivity, maintaining, 5
Ohtenjyou (*see* Tower tops and tower bottoms)
On-neck lines, 88, 91–93
On-neck lines combined, 91
Opening marubozu, 27
Opening prices, relationship between closing
    and, 7
Oracle Corp.
    dark cloud cover, 220
    dark cloud cover support/resistance,
        221–222
    dark cloud cover trade, 222–223
    dark cloud cover zoom out, 220–221
Osaka, Japan, 6
Oscillators, 177
    banded, 159, 170
    centered, 158
    MACD, 164
    rate of change, 169
    stochastic oscillator, 174

Pan American Silver Corp. (separating lines), 87
Patience, 224
Paychex Inc. (advance block), 111
Piercing line, 45–47, 167
Piercing line combined, 46
Piercing lines, 38
Plum Creek Timber Co. (10-day ROC trade),
    167
Point and figure charts, 17
Price gaps, 18 (*See also* Gaps)
Price(s)
    and technical analysis, 12
    relationship between opening and closing, 7
Pring, Martin J., 184

Protective sell stops, 85, 224
Psychology, trader, 6
Public Entertainment Group Inc.
    (three inside down), 70
Public Service Entertainment Group Inc.
    (three inside down), 71
Pullbacks, market, 143 (*See also* Retracements)

Quong, Gene, 193

Rate of change (ROC), 164–169, 178
    calculation of, 164–165
    simplicity of, 164
Rate (of price changes), 157
Raytheon Co.
    CMF, 200–201
    CMF trades, 200, 202
Real body, 24–25
Relative strength index (RSI), 174–177
Resistance (*see* Support and resistance)
Retracements, 150, 214
Reversal patterns, 74
    and market context, 57
    need to confirm, 38
    strong signal patterns, 57
    subtle patterns, 74
Rising and falling three methods, 96–99
Rising and falling three methods combined, 97
Rising windows, 19, 80
Risk, technical analysis and, 13, 15
ROC (*see* Rate of change)
RSI (*see* Relative strength index)
Runaway gaps, 152–153
Ryder Systems, Inc. (moving average support/
    resistance), 145

Sakata, Japan, 6
Sakata's strategies, 7, 73, 103–115
    significance of number three in, 115
    three gaps, 108–110
    three methods, 115
    three mountains, 104–107
    three rivers, 107–108
    three soldiers, 109–113
San-ku (*see* Three gaps)
Sanku fumiage (*see* Three upside gap strategy)

Sanku nage owari (*see* Three down gaps)
San-pei (*see* Three soldiers)
San-poh (*see* Three methods)
San-sen (*see* Three rivers)
San-zan (*see* Three mountains)
Scalping, 133
Select Sector Financial SPDR ETF
    (low price gapping play), 123, 124
Separating lines, 85–88
Shadows, 25, 29, (*See also* Marubozu lines)
Shaven bottom, 27
Shaven head, 27
Shinne hatte (*see* Eight new price lines)
Shooting star, 55, 167
Short candles, 27
Signal line, 159
Signal line crossovers, 162
Simple moving average, 133
Slow stochastic, 170
Soudack, Avrum, 193
Southwest Airlines Co. (exhaustion gap),
    153–154
SPDR Gold Trust ETF
    HLV indicator trades, 182
    VPP indicator, 203
SPDR S&P Retail ETF
    classic trend lines, 136, 138
Spinning tops, 29
Standard & Poor's (S&P) 500 Index, 2
    horizontal zones, 142–143
    value of (figure), 2
Stars, 32, 49–57
    defined, 49
    doji star, 53–54
    evening star, 51–53, 162
    inverted hammer, 54, 56
    morning star, 49–51
    shooting star, 54–55, 167
Stochastic oscillator, 169–174
Strong reversal patterns, 57
    dark cloud cover, 49
    engulfing patterns, 45
    hammer, 39–40
    hanging man, 41
    piercing line, 47
    stars, 57

Subtle reversal patterns, 74
    belt hold lines, 62
    harami, 60
    meeting lines, 67
    three black crows, 65
    three inside up and three inside down, 71
    three white soldiers, 64
    upside gap two crows, 69
Successful trades, making, 220
Supply and demand, technical analysis and, 12
Support and resistance, 139–150
    defined, 139
    horizontal lines/bands and, 140–144
    moving averages and, 145
    retracements and, 145–150
    significance of, 150
    trend lines and, 144–145
Support zones, 140

Tasuki gaps, 82–85, 113
Tasuki gaps combined, 83
Technical analysis, 20, 129–154
    and price, 12
    and risk, 13, 15
    defined, 11, 130
    fundamental analysis vs., 12, 15
    gaps in, 154
    goal of, 37
    mastering the art of, 15
    support/resistance in, 150
    trends in, 139
    value of, 129
    volume in, 12
    Western, 11
Technical Analysis from A to Z (Steven Achelis),
    161
Terminology, candlestick, 29
Terra Nitrogen Co. (resistance area), 142
Testing (of prior resistance area), 142
Texas Instruments, Inc. (hanging man pattern),
    39, 41
Three black crows, 64–65, 111–113
Three Buddha top, 105
Three down gaps, 109–110
Three gaps, 109
Three inside up and three inside down, 69–71

Three inside up and three inside down combined, 69

3M Corp.
   downside tasuki gap, 83

Three methods, 113–115

Three mountains, 107

Three outside up and three outside down, 71–73

Three outside up and three outside down combined, 72

Three rivers, 108

Three soldiers, 113

Three upside gap strategy, 108

Three white soldiers, 62–64, 109

Three-winged crow, 113

Thrusting lines, 93–96

Thrusting lines combined, 94

Titanium Metals Corp. (piercing line), 46–47

Tower tops and tower bottoms, 116–118

Trader (as term), 2

Trader psychology, 6

Trades and trading, 226
   bearish engulfing pattern example, 216–219
   bullish engulfing pattern example, 212–215
   checklist, trader's, 224
   dark cloud cover example, 220–224
   presentation of examples, 212
   successful trades, 219–220

Trend lines, 136–139, 145, 213

Trend(s), 130–139
   defined, 130
   moving averages in, 131–136
   neutral, 132
   up- vs. down-, 130

Triple bottom, 107

Tweezer tops and tweezer bottoms, 120–122

Two-winged crow, 113

Umbrella lines, 33

United Parcel Service Inc. (internal retracement levels), 147–148

Upper shadow, 25

Upside gap three method, 113–114

Upside gap two crows, 67–69

Upside gap two crows combined, 68

Upside tasuki gap, 84

Uptrends, 130, 139

U.S. Dollar Index (fry pan bottom), 120

U.S. Federal Reserve, 143

V bottom, 116

Velocity (of price changes), 157

Verizon Communications
   VPP indicator support and resistance, 204
   VPP indicator trades, 205

Volatility, 134

Volume
   and accumulation/distribution (AD) line, 195–198
   and Chaikin AD oscillator, 198–200
   and Chaikin money flow, 200–202
   and money flow index, 193–195
   and short candles, 27
   in technical analysis, 12
   limitations of analyzing, 192
   patterns in, 188–193
   value of analyzing, 188
   when not to trust, 190

Volume percent positive (VPP), 202–206, 212

V top, 116

Walt Disney Co. (trend line support/resistance), 144

Western technical analysis, 11

Whipsaw signals, 159–160

White marubozu, 27

White *sanpei* (*see* Three white soldiers)

Wicks (*see* Shadows)

Width (of real body), 24

Wilder, J. Welles, 174

Windows, 18, 80–85

Wynn Resorts Inc.
   bearish engulfing pattern, 216
   bearish engulfing pattern retracement and divergence, 217–218
   bearish engulfing pattern trade, 218–219
   bearish engulfing pattern zoom out, 216–217

Zero line crossovers, 159